The Dynamics of Organizational Levels

The Dynamics of Organizational Levels

A Change Framework for Managers and Consultants

Nicholas S. Rashford
St. Joseph's University
Philadelphia

David Coghlan
The National College of Industrial Relations
Dublin, Ireland

ADDISON-WESLEY PUBLISHING COMPANY
Reading, Massachusetts • Menlo Park, California • New York
Don Mills, Ontario • Wokingham, England • Amsterdam • Bonn
Sydney • Singapore • Tokyo • Madrid • San Juan • Milan • Paris

Library of Congress Cataloging-in-Publication Data

Rashford, Nicholas S.
   The dynamics of organizational levels : a change framework for
managers and consultants / Nicholas S. Rashford. David Coghlan.
      p.   cm. -- (Addison-Wesley series on organizational
   development)
   Includes bibliographical references.
   ISBN 0-201-54323-0
   1. Organizational change.   2. Communication in organizations.
I. Coghlan, David. II. Title. III. Series.
HD58.8.R35   1993
658.4'06--dc20   93-14814
                                                               CIP

Reprinted with corrections, December 1993.
This book is in the Addison-Wesley Series on Organization Development.
Editors: Edgar H. Schein, Richard Beckhard

ISBN 0-201-54323-0
2 3 4 5 6 7 8 9 10-BA-97969594

In memory of our mothers, Brigid and Augusta,
who died during the writing of this book

Other Titles in the Organization Development Series

Competing with Flexible Lateral Organizations, Second Edition

Jay R. Galbraith

1994 (50836)

This book focuses on creating competitive advantage by building a lateral capability, enabling a firm to respond flexibly in an uncertain world. The book addresses international coordination and cross business coordination as well as the usual cross functional efforts. It is unique in covering both cross functional (lateral or horizontal) coordination, as well as international and corporate issues.

Organization Development: A Process of Learning and Changing, Second Edition

W. Warner Burke

1994 (50835)

This text presents an overview of OD and looks at OD in part as a change of an organization's culture. It looks at the organization and factors that will influence structure and development in the future. The author also introduces new topics such as information management and strategy implementation.

Total Quality: A User's Guide for Implementation

Dan Ciampa

1992 (54992)

This is a book that directly addresses the challenge of how to make Total Quality work in a practical, no-nonsense way. The companies that will dominate markets in the future will be those that deliver high quality, competitively priced products and service just when the customer wants them and in a way that exceeds the customer's expectations. The vehicle by which these companies move to that stage is Total Quality.

Parallel Learning Structures: Increasing Innovation in Bureaucracies

Gervase R. Bushe and A.B. Shani

1991 (52427)

Parallel learning structures are technostructural interventions that promote system-wide change in bureaucracies while retaining the advantages of bureaucratic design. This text serves as a resource of models and theories built around five cases of parallel learning structures that can help those who create and maintain them be more effective and successful. For those new to parallel learning structures, the text provides practical advice as to when and how to use them.

Managing in the New Team Environment: Skills, Tools, and Methods
Larry Hirschhorn
1991 (52503)
This text is designed to help manage the tensions and complexities that arise for managers seeking to guide employees in a team environment. Based on an interactive video course developed at IBM, the text takes managers step by step through the process of building a team and authorizing it to act while they learn to step back and delegate. Specific issues addressed are how to give a team structure, how to facilitate its basic processes, and how to acknowledge differences in relationships among team members and between the manager and individual team members.

Leading Business Teams: How Teams Can Use Technology and Group Process Tools to Enhance Performance
Robert Johansen, David Sibbett, Suzyn Benson, Alexia Martin, Robert Mittman, and Paul Saffo
1991 (52829)
What technology or tools should organization development people or team leaders have at their command, now and in the future? This text explores the intersection of technology and business teams, a new and largely uncharted area that goes by several labels, including "groupware," a term that encompasses both electronic and nonelectronic tools for teams. This is the first book of its kind from the field describing what works for business teams and what does not.

The Conflict-Positive Organization: Stimulate Diversity and Create Unity
Dean Tjosvold
1991 (51485)
This book describes how managers and employees can use conflict to find common ground, solve problems, and strengthen morale and relationships. By showing how well-managed conflict invigorates and empowers teams and organizations, the text demonstrates how conflict is vital for a company's continuous improvement and increased competitive advantage.

Change by Design

Robert R. Blake, Jane Srygley Mouton, and Anne Adams McCanse

1989 (50748)

This book develops a systematic approach to organization development and provides readers with rich illustrations of coherent planned change. The book involves testing, examining, revising, and strengthening conceptual foundations in order to create sharper corporate focus and increased predictability of successful organization development.

Organization Development in Health Care

R. Wayne Boss

1989 (18364)

This is the first book to discuss the intricacies of the health care industry. The book explains the impact of OD in creating healthy and viable organizations in the health care sector. Through unique and innovative techniques, hospitals are able to reduce nursing turnover, thereby resolving the nursing shortage problem. The text also addresses how OD can improve such bottom-line variables as cash flow and net profits.

Self-Designing Organizations: Learning How to Create High Performance

Susan Albers Mohrman and Thomas G. Cummings

1989 (14603)

This book looks beyond traditional approaches to organizational transition, offering a strategy for developing organizations that enables them to learn not only how to adjust to the dynamic environment in which they exist, but also how to achieve a higher level of performance. This strategy assumes that change is a learning process: the goal is continually refined as organizational members learn how to function more effectively and respond to dynamic conditions in their environment.

Power and Organization Development: Mobilizing Power to Implement Change

Larry E. Greiner and Virginia E. Schein

1988 (12185)

This book forges an important collaborative approach between two opposing and often contradictory approaches to management: OD practitioners who espouse a "more humane" workplace without understanding the political realities of getting things done, and practicing managers who feel comfortable with power but overlook the role of human potential in contributing to positive results.

Designing Organizations for High Performance
David P. Hanna

1988 (12693)

This book is the first to give insight into the actual processes you can use to translate organizational concepts into bottom-line improvements. Hanna's "how-to" approach shows not only the successful methods of intervention, but also the plans behind them and the corresponding results.

Process Consultation, Volume 1: Its Role in Organization Development, Second Edition
Edgar H. Schein

1988 (06736)

How can a situation be influenced in the workplace without the direct use of power or formal authority? This book presents the core theoretical foundations and basic prescriptions for effective management.

Organizational Transitions: Managing Complex Change, Second Edition
Richard Beckhard and Reuben T. Harris

1987 (10887)

This book discusses the choices involved in developing a management system appropriate to the "transition state." It also discusses commitment to change, organizational culture, and increasing and maintaining productivity, creativity, and innovation.

Organization Development: A Normative View
W. Warner Burke

1987 (10697)

This book concisely describes and defines the theories and practices of organization development and also looks at organization development as change in an organization's culture. It is a useful guide to the field of organization development and is invaluable to managers, executives, practitioners, and anyone desiring an excellent overview of this multi-faceted field.

Team Building: Issues and Alternatives, Second Edition
William G. Dyer

1987 (18037)

Through the use of the techniques and procedures described in this book, managers and consultants can effectively prepare, apply, and follow up on the human processes affecting the productive functioning of teams.

The Technology Connection: Strategy and Change in the Information Age
Marc S. Gerstein

1987 (12188)

This is a book that guides managers and consultants through crucial decisions about the use of technology for increasing effectiveness and competitive advantage. It provides a useful way to think about the relationship between information technology, business strategy, and the process of change in organizations.

Stream Analysis: A Powerful Way to Diagnose and Manage Organizational Change
Jerry I. Porras

1987 (05693)

Drawing on a conceptual framework that helps the reader to better understand organizations, this book shows how to diagnose failings in organizational functioning and how to plan a comprehensive set of actions needed to change the organization into a more effective system.

Process Consultation, Volume II: Lessons for Managers and Consultants
Edgar H. Schein

1987 (06744)

This book shows the viability of the process consultation model for working with human systems. Like Schein's first volume on process consultation, the second volume focuses on the moment-to-moment behavior of the manager or consultant rather than on the design of the OD program.

Managing Conflict: Interpersonal Dialogue and Third-Party Roles, Second Edition
Richard E. Walton

1987 (08859)

This book shows how to implement a dialogue approach to conflict management. It presents a framework for diagnosing recurring conflicts and suggests several basic options for controlling or resolving them.

Pay and Organization Development
Edward E. Lawler

1981 (03990)

This book examines the important role that reward systems play in organization development efforts. By combining examples and specific recommendations with conceptual material, it organizes the various topics and puts them into a total systems perspective. Specific pay approaches such as gainsharing, skill-based pay, and flexible benefits are discussed and their impact on productivity and the quality of work life is analyzed.

Work Redesign
J. Richard Hackman and Greg R. Oldham
1980 (02779)

This book is a comprehensive, clearly written study of work design as a strategy for personal and organizational change. Linking theory and practical technologies, it develops traditional and alternative approaches to work design that can benefit both individuals and organizations.

Organizational Dynamics: Diagnosis and Intervention
John P. Kotter
1978 (03890)

This book offers managers and OD specialists a powerful method of diagnosing organizational problems and of deciding when, where, and how to use (or not use) the diverse and growing number of organizational improvement tools that are available today. Comprehensive and fully integrated, the book includes many different concepts, research findings, and competing philosophies and provides specific examples of how to use the information to improve organizational functioning.

Career Dynamics: Matching Individual and Organizational Needs
Edgar H. Schein
1978 (06834)

This book studies the complexities of career development from both an individual and an organizational perspective. Changing needs throughout the adult life cycle, interaction of work and family, and integration of individual and organizational goals through human resource planning and development are all thoroughly explored.

Matrix
Stanley M. Davis and Paul Lawrence
1977 (01115)

This book defines and describes the matrix organization, a significant departure from the traditional "one man-one boss" management system. The author notes that the tension between the need for independence (fostering innovation) and order (fostering efficiency) drives organizations to consider a matrix system. Among the issues addressed are reasons for using a matrix, methods for establishing one, the impact of the system on individuals, its hazards, and what types of organizations can use a matrix system.

Feedback and Organization Development: Using Data-Based Methods

David A. Nadler

1977 (05006)

This book addresses the use of data as a tool for organizational change. It attempts to bring together some of what is known from experience and research and to translate that knowledge into useful insights for those who are thinking about using data-based methods in organizations. The broad approach of the text is to treat a whole range of questions and issues considering the various uses of data as an organizational change tool.

Designing Complex Organizations

Jay Galbraith

1973 (02559)

This book attempts to present an analytical framework of the design of organizations, particularly of types of organizations that apply lateral decision processes or matrix forms. These forms have become pervasive in all types of organizations, yet there is little systematic public knowledge about them. This book helps fill this gap.

Organization Development: Strategies and Models

Richard Beckhard

1969 (00448)

This book is written for managers, specialists, and students of management who are concerned with the planning of organization development programs to resolve the dilemmas brought about by a rapidly changing environment. Practiced teams of interdependent people must spend real time improving their methods of working, decision making, and communicating, and a planned, managed change is the first step toward effecting and maintaining these improvements.

Organization Development: Its Nature, Origins, and Prospects

Warren G. Bennis

1969 (00523)

This primer on OD is written with an eye toward the people in organizations who are interested in learning more about this educational strategy as well as for those practitioners and students of OD who may want a basic statement both to learn from and to argue with. The author treats the subject with a minimum of academic jargon and a maximum of concrete examples drawn from his own and others' experience.

Developing Organizations: Diagnosis and Action
Paul R. Lawrence and Jay W. Lorsch

1969 (04204)

This book is a personal statement of the authors' evolving experience, through research and consulting, in the work of developing organizations. The text presents the authors' overview of organization development, then proceeds to examine issues at each of three critical interfaces: the organization-environment interface, the group-group interface, and the individual-organization interface, including brief examples of work on each. The text concludes by pulling the themes together in a set of conclusions about organizational development issues as they present themselves to practicing managers.

About the Authors

Nicholas S. Rashford is President of St. Joseph's University, Philadelphia, and was formerly Dean of the School of Management, Rockhurst College, Kansas City. He has an S.M. in management from MIT's Sloan School of Management, where he was a Sloan Fellow, and an Sc.D. in behavioral science in medicine from Johns Hopkins University. He has initiated the development of the concept of organizational levels, used widely in teaching and consulting, and with David Coghlan, published applications to OD, management training and education, university administration, religious ministry, and organizational change. He currently chairs the Delaware River Port Authority and is Commissioner of the Philadelphia Regional Port Authority.

David Coghlan teaches at the National College of Industrial Relations, Dublin, Ireland. He has an M.Sc. in management science from the University of Manchester Institute of Science and Technology and an S.M. in management from MIT's Sloan School of Management, where he was a Sloan Fellow. He has published more than fifty articles in such journals as *Leadership & Organization Development Journal, Journal of Managerial Psychology, Long Range Planning, Person-Centered Review,* and the *Organizational Behavior Teaching Review.* He has a particular interest in the application of strategic management and organization development to church and religious systems, works as an OD consultant in that area, and has published extensively on that subject.

Foreword

The Addison-Wesley Series on Organization Development originated in the late 1960s when a number of us recognized that the rapidly growing field of "OD" was not well understood or well defined. We also recognized that there was no one OD philosophy, and hence one could not at that time write a textbook on the theory and practice of OD, but one could make clear what various practitioners were doing under that label. So the original six books launched what has since become a continuing enterprise, the essence of which was to allow different authors to speak for themselves instead of trying to summarize under one umbrella what was obviously a rapidly growing and highly diverse field.

By the early 1980s the series included nineteen titles. OD was growing by leaps and bounds, and it was expanding into all kinds of organizational areas and technologies of intervention. By this time, many textbooks existed as well that tried to capture core concepts of the field, but we felt that diversity and innovation were still the more salient aspects of OD.

Now as we move into the 1990s our series includes over thirty titles, and we are beginning to see some real convergence in the underlying assumptions of OD. As we observe how different professionals working in different kinds of organizations and occupational communities make their case, we see we are still far from having a single "theory" of organization development. Yet, a set of common assumptions is surfacing. We are beginning to see patterns in what works and what does not work, and we are becoming more articulate about these patterns. We are also seeing the field increasingly connected to other organizational sciences and disciplines such as information technology, coordination theory, and organization theory. In the early 1990s we saw several important themes described with Ciampa's *Total Quality* showing the important link to employee involvement in continuous improvement, Johansen et al.'s *Leading Business Teams* exploring the important arena of electronic information tools for teamwork, Tjosvold's *The Conflict-Positive Organization* showing how conflict management can turn conflict into constructive action, Hirschhorn's *Managing in the New Team Environment* building bridges to group psychodynamic theory, and Bushe and Shani's *Parallel Learning Structures* providing an integrative theory for large-scale organization change.

We continue this trend with two revisions and one wholly new approach. Burke has taken his highly successful *Organization Development* into new realms with an updating and expansion. Galbraith has updated and enlarged his classic theory of how information management is at the heart of organization design with his new edition entitled *Competing with Flexible Lateral Organizations,* and Rashford and Coghlan have introduced the important concept of levels of organizational complexity as a basis for intervention theory in their book entitled *The Dynamics of Organizational Levels.*

We welcome these revisions and new titles and will continue to explore the various frontiers of organization development with additional titles as we identify themes that are relevant to the ever more difficult problem of helping organizations to remain effective in an increasingly turbulent environment.

New York, New York   Richard H. Beckhard
Cambridge, Massachusetts   Edgar H. Schein

Preface

The origins of a friendship are often difficult to reconstruct. A team development workshop in Ireland in 1975, in which Nicholas Rashford was a staff member and David Coghlan a participant, was certainly our initial contact. Meeting a year later, again for a similar workshop, led to a mentorship. In the subsequent years, Nicholas invited David to teach at Rockhurst College, Kansas City, and persuaded him to follow his footsteps in the Alfred P. Sloan Fellows Program at MIT's Sloan School of Management. From there the mentorship grew to colleagueship and friendship and many occasions when we conducted workshops, co-taught executive MBA classes, and spent many hours discussing ideas. Our shared experiences of the MIT Sloan School of Management (separated by twelve years) gave us a common conceptual framework, particularly through Ed Schein's writings and teaching.

From our teaching, training, and consulting over the years, we have found that an individual's personal experience in an organization has an effect on how he or she participates in a team, and that a team's dynamics affect the way the individual perceives his or her role in the organization. We notice that decisions made at the corporate strategic level have an impact on the coordination of information and resources within an organization, which in turn, affects what happens in a particular team or department, which, in turn, affects individuals' perceptions and motivation.

In general, these interrelationships do not receive much coverage in the organization development literature. When we have turned to the books for encouragement and inspiration in difficult consulting experiences, we have found little there to help us understand whether an individual's dysfunctional behavior that is blocking a team's process is the individual's own issue or one engendered by that very team. As we struggled with individual clients' disaffection with corporate strategic decisions, we came to see that dynamic relationships exist among individuals, teams, groups of teams, and organizations. These relationships are the lifeblood of the change process in any organization.

The term *organizational levels* can be used to mean different things. It typically refers to positions on the hierarchical ladder. In organization development texts it frequently describes types of interventions: individual, group, or organizational. We use the term to describe levels of complexity and interdependence, in other words, how an individual and an organization relate, how a team functions, how a group of teams is coordinated, how an organization attempts to survive in its external environment, and how each of these processes affects the others.

This book is our attempt to share with managers, consultants, and teachers of organizational behavior some of our insights on such complex organizational dynamics. We hope that our reflections on our experience and the accompanying conceptualization into a comprehensive framework will demonstrate that the construct of organizational levels is essential for anyone who wishes to understand and work with organizations.

Acknowledgments

Writing a book across a 5000 mile distance has been difficult and exciting for both of us. It has been challenging to draw together into a single volume the concepts and frameworks of our shared publications, training, consulting, and teaching.

We are grateful for permission from MCB University Press to publish developed versions of previously published articles. An earlier version of Chapter 2 appeared in *Leadership & Organization Development Journal* (Vol. 8, 1987, No. 1, 17–21); of Chapter 6 in *The Journal of Managerial Psychology* (Vol. 4, 1989, No. 3, 17–22); and of Chapter 8 in *Leadership & Organization Development Journal* (Vol. 8, 1987, No. 3, 3–8).

We both acknowledge that our students and clients have contributed significantly to the developing and refining over the years of the construct of four organizational levels. Students at Loyola College, Baltimore; Rockhurst College, Kansas City; Saint Joseph's University, Philadelphia; The National College of Industrial Relations, Dublin; University College, Dublin; and many clients in business, government, health, educational, voluntary, and church organizations have asked key questions and made invaluable suggestions as to how to apply the framework to their own organizations.

Helping people and systems change requires a disposition and skills grounded in an intellectual formation that, for us, has come from the experience of working with established practitioners. The conceptual insights of this book would not be realized in practice without the practical learning from mentors and colleagues. Nicholas thanks particularly Howard Head, Erivan Karl Haub, and the many other entrepreneurs who revealed what it means to conceive an idea and develop it into a business. He also thanks Tom Lyon, and the other faculty members of Rockhurst College, and Dick Beckhard as a teacher and mentor. David acknowledges his debt to Philip Harnett, who changed his life by introducing him to experiential learning, group facilitation, and his library, and provided many occasions for putting theory and learning into practice; to Richard Ottaway, who generated and fostered an excitement about Kurt Lewin, the theory and practice of planned change, and in particular the study of the change agent, and to Eddie McIlduff, whose person-centered approach is a support and challenge to remain grounded in the core values of a respect for the individual's autonomy.

There are many colleagues and friends whose contribution we wish to acknowledge. Some have given much needed personal support; some have contributed to the formulation of ideas; others have helped with production of the book by reading drafts and giving feedback or providing technological assistance. David thanks Teresa Brannick, Colette O'Sullivan, Richard Ottaway, Anne Regan, Patrick Riordan, Sean Ruth, Bill Toner, and David Tuohy. Nicholas thanks Helen Stewart, Joe Chorpenning, Dave Dore, Steve Porth, and the Executive Masters' Class at Saint Joseph's University.

We are both particularly indebted to Ed Schein. For many years he has played a key role in the development of our conceptual and practical frameworks—through his writings, as our teacher in the MIT Sloan School of Management, and especially as the editor of this book. He has supported and challenged us to have confidence in our ideas and to stay with them, to clarify our thoughts and their expression, and to take them to publication.

Philadelphia, Pennsylvania   N.S.R.
Dublin, Ireland   D.C.

Contents

1

A New Perspective
on Organizations

Levels within an organization is a concept typically used to describe steps on an organization's hierarchical ladder. When people speak of the level of management they occupy, they mean their location on the organizational chart. Less commonly, organizational levels refers to levels of complexity, such as the individual, the team, the interdepartmental group or function consisting of many teams, and the total organization. We propose that the latter way of conceiving organizational levels is especially relevant to managers and organization development (OD) practitioners. The method focuses on four complex areas that occur in every organization: (1) the individual's relationship with the organization and the organization's relationship with the individual, (2) the way teams function, (3) coordination of the teams that make up departments and larger units of the organization, and (4) the way the organization as a whole adapts to its environment. This way of defining levels also helps us to focus on the dynamic interrelationships between the different levels of complexity, such as the effect of the individual on the organization and vice versa, the relationship between individual and team or between team and interdepartmental group, the internal organization of departments, and the organization's interaction with the external environment. These relationships and their systemic context are not given much consideration in the literature on organizational behavior, change, and development. Yet they are very common and critical issues in OD consulting work.

For OD consultants, teachers of organizational behavior, trainers, or managers, a framework of organizational levels that describes the tasks of the individual, the team, the interdepartmental group, and the organization and articulates their interrelationships and interdependencies is essential. As the cases that follow demonstrate, the organizational levels' paradigm provides a useful insight into the way change takes place in organizations.

The concept of levels of complexity first emerged as one of us, Nicholas Rashford, was teaching an MBA class of managers a course on business policy. Considering the area of focus for a manger in complex business situations, it became clear to him that managers need to understand individuals and their motivation, team function and repair, the complex aspects of interdepartmental group and function interplay, and finally, the outcome state of an organization acting alone in a more complex environment with other organizations.

The MBA class at Loyola University, Baltimore, convened its business policy course in fall 1973. It was his first time teaching a course at the college level and Rashford was (understandably) nervous about undertaking the project. Wishing to bring some of his experience of the Sloan executive program at MIT to bear, he incorporated theories of organization development and process consultation into the course. He assigned as texts Schein's *Process Consultation,* Beckhard's *Organization Development: Strategies and Models,* and the Harvard Business School case study book. It was in discussing the confluence of these three streams—the case method, organization development, and process consultation—that he first saw clearly that three or four different organizational behavioral concepts were interlinked and essential for managers to grasp in order to solve complex problems.

The class itself was a microcosm of a complex situation. Each student had made a decision to deepen his or her own experiential base at a career midpoint. Each had come to this particular class in order to develop the skills, self-esteem, and confidence needed to move to a higher, more encompassing management position. These skills would enhance the student/managers' value to and strengthen their bonding with their respective organizations.

The wisdom or sense to choose to return to the classroom to improve themselves was different from the knowledge and skills necessary to work together in a class effort to solve cases as a team or to work together as a management group to decide how to implement strategy or policy in a business or other organization. The class as a discrete organizational group had to learn to work with a particular teacher. The dual skills of working with an external force (the teacher) and of interacting in a student group were very different organizational skills from those of managing their careers and forming a team.

As a unit working on cases the class of managers and managers-to-be simulated situations they faced in everyday life. The perspective of the organization adapting as a unit in a competitive environment—the heart of the course—differed again from the individual behaviors and choices of the key players and from the management team behavior. It was within this context that the concept of levels was born. How do you teach the analysis and understanding of behaviors necessary to make complex decisions? The behavioral experience of role-playing the cases, when understood, would provide the basis for the answer.

The levels can also be understood in terms of four modes of participation: *Level I,* the individual mode, is the interaction of the individual in a contract to belong and to be a part of an organization. *Level II* is the interaction of a member of an organization with others working in a face-to-face team to accomplish more complex tasks. *Level III* is the interaction of interdepartmental groups or functional units or intraorganization groups to produce complex products or services within an organization. *Level IV* is the total organization's action as a single unit. This fourth level is a mode of behavior, because when an organization interacts with its competition as a unit, its competition reacts, which in turn necessitates further action by the original organization. For an organization to tap the full potential of the human resource, it must enable its participants or operate in four distinct modes or on all four of these levels.

The levels concept is illustrated in the experience of Head Ski Company. As Rashford became closely acquainted with Howard Head, he learned how the major events in that company's history could best be understood in terms of the four levels of organizational complexity. Wanting to discuss real behavior in the course, Rashford had been pleased to note that the first case in the textbook, Head Ski Company, was located in Baltimore and he wondered whether founder Howard Head lived nearby. A quick scan of the telephone directory confirmed that he did. Head agreed to come to the class, and eventually became a friend. During the class, the students role-played the Head Ski case, not knowing that one of the guests observing the process was Howard Head.

The Failure of a Successful Company

CASE: Howard Head was born in Philadelphia and educated at Harvard, where he studied engineering science in a liberal arts based program. After graduation Head returned to Philadelphia, where he worked for *The Philadelphia Bulletin* reporting on science and technology. Dissatisfied with the career of a reporter, Head applied to the Martin Company in the early war years. Working there with people like J. S. McDonnell, Don Douglas, and L. F. Martin, he developed his skills as an engineer as he furthered his studies and technical experience in the area of aluminum manufacturing and fabrication.

Head's curiosity was legendary. He was constantly trying to decipher how things worked. Not satisfied with that, he also tried to figure out ways to make them better. At the Martin Company he worked on the design of aircraft fuel tanks and looked for other ways to use aluminum. One of his favorite pastimes being skiing, which he pursued each season on the slopes of New England, he concluded that ski design could be revolutionized by making skis of aluminum instead of wood, the traditional material. Head Ski Company was born in Howard Head's basement, as he began to work on this challenging innovation.

Head's fascination with aluminum grew. His work at the Martin Company centered on building the internal cavities in aircraft to be used in carrying fuel, which were honeycombed so that the fuel would not explode in the event of a crash. At home he employed honeycombed aluminum fabricating skis that would perform better. Head took the rough fabricated aluminum skis to Mount Washington in New Hampshire to try them out himself and to talk professional skiers into doing the same thing. After much trial and error, he was able to bond the bottom of a ski to a honeycomb middle layer that gave it the strength and flexibility necessary to react better than any other configuration to the stresses of twisting and bending during skiing on snow.

Head was very enthusiastic about this breakthrough. Many skis had broken because the aluminum tended to become brittle in the cold and snap. After about 130 different pairs had been tested in one way or another, a professional skier agreed to test the newest configuration of skis Head had brought to the mountains. He went to the top of the slope and flew down in a beautiful ski run. Head likens his elation at this moment to having given birth. He stood in thrilled admiration as his skis were put to their ultimate test by a professional athlete who could now ski better than ever before.

Building skis in Timonium, Maryland, was a backroom operation of cutting, grinding, and amalgamating strips of aluminum into a compact ski. Adhesives, glues, and other materials were used in the process, and the manufacturing engineering was as exciting to Howard Head as the building of the original skis. The entire manufacturing and assembly took place in four rooms. Skis were made all year and stored for selling in the winter. Over the next fifteen years Head Ski Company grew, moved to larger headquarters, and developed into a full-scale, though small and elite, ski company. It faced all the critical problems typical of an entrepreneurial company at this point in its existence. Equity grew slowly because it was limited to the return from profitability plowed back into the company each year. A critical market factor for the ski industry is that skis tend to be sold during only three or four months of the year. Skis built during the rest of the year have to be stored as inventory until the selling season, thus resulting in a low turnover of inventory and a high cost of furnished goods. Having pushed the company's bank loans to the extreme, Head sought some limited investors.

The investment group provided new capital that helped the ski company to carry on its work until once again it neared an upper limit. Tired of running the company by that time, Head hired a general manager, Harold Siegal, who had been managing a firm that specialized in the manufacture of electronic products for radio. Siegal was interested in the job with Head Ski Company because he could be CEO, operate the company for Howard Head, and bring mainstream management practices to it.

His first task was to address two major problems facing the company. The first was the length of time required to fabricate a ski. The longest single process was the bonding together of the different layers under an extremely heavy press. The seven hours to complete this step was a constraint that severely curtailed the number of skis the plant could produce at one time. Siegal put the bonding process on a twenty-four-hour shift and speeded it up by introducing pressurized bonding, a method he believed would be as good as the old method. Soon after skis fabricated by this new technique reached the market, however, complaints began to reach the company. The bottoms of the skis were falling off! Ski professionals protested the firm's inadequate quality control and the industry wondered what was happening to the prestigious Head Skis.

The second problem general manager Siegal faced was the insufficiency of equity already alluded to. There was no way to overcome the problem of high inventory necessitated by the short selling season. Consequently new equity was required for the company. Attracting new equity would mean a reduction of the proportion of equity held by Howard Head. After a long battle with Head, shareholders finally voted to seek a larger number of investors through a public stock offering. Realizing he was no longer the principal shareholder, Head requested that his share be purchased.

After buying out Head's shares, the Head Ski Company continued on its own for a short time. But Head Ski once again found itself short of capital and was unable to meet its production needs. A suitor was identified in the AMF Company, which purchased the Head Ski Company, including its name and patents. Labor problems ensued shortly because the unions had worked directly with Head in a close relationship. When AMF came in and won production gains and other concessions in their negotiations with the union, the workers went on strike. AMF took the patents, closed down the company in Maryland, and started a whole new production line within their own facilities in Colorado Springs. All the original employees ceased to work for Head Ski Company, and the equipment was sold off.

This is not the end of Howard Head, as we shall in a further case. After stepping back from Head Ski Company, Head took up a new sport—tennis. Fascinated with a tennis ball throwing machine he had purchased for tennis practice and then redesigned, he invested in the small company that manufactured the machine. His involvement with this firm, the Prince Company, became the basis for Head's designing a revolutionary new tennis racquet and for the second time, developing a highly popular product and a thriving company and industry leader. As we progress through our discussion of the levels framework, we will return to Head Ski Company for further analysis as well as to the Prince Company, which came later in Howard Head's career, and finally, we will compare the two.

Analysis of the Head Ski Case Through Organizational Levels

The Head Ski case can be examined through the four different lenses of organizational levels. At the individual level, it is obvious the Head Ski Company was very much an extension of Howard Head's own personality and background. His broad-based education at Harvard was supplemented by the technical knowledge he gained by working in the aircraft industry, specifically knowledge of aluminum, the material he came to know best. His avocational or recreational interests led to his desire to make the best skis possible. His personality and interests were manifested in a strong technical orientation for the company he founded. The company's engineering division was an extension of Head, himself the chief designer and engineer of the skis, the tools, and the surrounding machinery. He was as proud of the machinery as he was of the skis, but the machinery was good only if the skis were the best in the world.

Staying close to the sales force was also critical to Howard Head. The sales force represented an interface between Head and the professionals, whom Head knew and admired. Professional skiers were the best source of feedback on the effectiveness of the skis and on the success of his ability to produce the best skis in the world.

Harold Siegal, the general manager Head hired, had a different perspective. He was committed to a management structure in which he would be the key player. It was an organization driven by efficiency and the ability to turn a technical product into something the consumer would buy and use. Siegal had a real interest in making the sales force the marketing force of the company and felt that the engineering could be left to Head. Success for Siegal was an effective organization manufacturing the greatest number of skis and returning the greatest profitability on those skis. Success for Head was praise from the professionals for the best skis possible. These two views of the organization were bound to clash.

On the team level, it becomes obvious that the view of the organization Siegal brought to the company needed to mesh with Head's view. This did not happen. There was little chance of a functioning, working team; it was impossible for the two of them to talk through the roles and to have a productive face-to-face interaction. When the role descriptions were set down, Head was to be responsible for the engineering function, while Siegal was to manage the overall company. When the bottoms fell off the skis, Head was frustrated and angry at Siegal. He reassumed the role of CEO, frustrating Siegal by his interference. The face-to-face team comprising Head and Siegal ceased to function at this point.

At the interdepartmental level, or interfunctional level, there was a classical failure to cooperate and interact. The sales department was driven by its interactions with the professional skiers and wanted a high-quality product. The engineering function allied itself with sales. The engineers were under Head's direction, and they too wanted a superior product. The marketing group, on the other hand, wanted to sell as many skis as possible. The marketing force allied itself with the production department, which was trying to cut corners and increase productivity. These two functions were headed by Siegal. The two camps—production and marketing on one side, and sales and engineering on the other—came into face-to-face confrontation when the product broke down. Interdepartmental dysfunction is typical of many organizations and is poorly understood.

At the organizational level, when Head Ski Company sought to increase its capitalization by a public offering of stock to private investors, Head's ownership was diluted. He abandoned his commitment to the organization when his stock was bought out. At the same time the company also faced a challenge from manufacturers of fiberglass skis. Head Ski had developed the technology in manufacturing aluminum skis. It had some of the best aluminum engineers in the country applying their skills to skis; the manufacturing process was set up to shape, bond, and fabricate an aluminum product. No one in the company, including the founder and CEO, had any interest, knowledge, or background in fiberglass. The company's investment in an aluminum product made a shift to fiberglass unlikely. The market was changing, a new opportunity existed, but fiberglass skis would never be developed by the Head Ski Company.

Organizational Levels as the Basis for OD Intervention

A superficial look at the Head Ski case would indicate that it is a marketing-finance case, but closer examination reveals it to be the Level II dysfunction that created the basic problem in the company, which is comprehensible by understanding Head's relationship with the organization.

Analyzing the issues at the four organizational levels can provide the basis for possible interventions by an OD consultant. The most basic place to intervene is Level I. On this level the detailed versions of what both Head and Siegal respectively thought the company ought to be would be explained. A Level II intervention subsequently would entail sitting them down to work toward an agreement that would accommodate their respective views of the value of the organization. Such an intervention would be preparatory to building a face-to-face team. Both Head's and Siegal's roles would be defined in such a way as to set up a forum for resolution of conflict. As it was, no such forum existed, and the leaders' contradicting roles were never challenged. The ultimate effect was to introduce discord at the interdepartmental group level. A team with Head and Siegal working together could have responded to the crucial information the sales force was reporting: that the skis were falling apart and the reputation of the company was being tarnished. This information should have flowed back to production where the corner-cutting exercise would have been curtailed and the honor of both product and company saved. An intervention focusing on interdepartmental relations would have been appropriate.

At the organizational level, Level IV, an intervention would have focused on how capital and the financial implications of ownership directly affect a small organization in the entrepreneurial phase of its life cycle. In attempting to sort out the financial implications and the effects on the organization at this level, a consultant would assess the value of the basic commitment of the key individual, Howard Head. If Head's expertise were to be undercut by diluting his share of the stock and leaving him less than majority ownership, then an alternative stock offering needed to be designed. Intervention at Level IV would have enabled the board of directors, Head, and the investors to see the cost of Head's departure and compare it with the gains, the increased funds for expansion. This intervention and a positive response from the board could have adverted the final outcome, which was Head's departure from the organization and the dissolution of the company.

A further Level IV intervention would have been required a short time later because of the materials change in the ski industry. Head Ski Company's refusal to shift from aluminum to fiberglass would have to be challenged if the company were to continue its success despite a changed environment.

Viewing OD interventions in terms of the four levels also points to the essential interrelationships between the levels. If individuals do not bond well to the organization they do not form effective teams; without effective teams interdepartmental coordination becomes more difficult; and without such coordination the organization cannot formulate and execute a viable strategy.

Summary

We've begun this book by providing an initial description of the construct of organizational levels. A background in case work and organization development is enhanced by a use of levels theory in understanding not only the Head Ski case but all organizational change and development cases. The organizational levels framework can be used by both the manager and the external consultant. From their own perspectives, each attempts to see what is happening in the organization, understand why it is happening, and take appropriate action. The organizational levels construct helps unravel the multiple complex issues that occur in organizations.

Plan of the Book

This book is about understanding the dynamics of each organizational level and the relation of each level to the others. We define "levels" as *levels of participation* in order to distinguish the term from another use and definition, as steps on an organization's hierarchy.

Level I is the individual level, whereby the individual member and the organization attempt a bonding relationship.

Level II is the face-to-face team level, whereby individuals engage in working with others as a functioning team.

Level III is the interdepartmental group level in which multiple teams form a coordinated effort.

Level IV is the organizational level by which an organization adapts proactively to the demands of its external environment.

These four levels will be defined and explained in Chapter 2. Chapter 3 presents a framework for focusing interventions on each level. Chapter 4 shows how the four levels are interlinked. Chapter 5 introduces the topic of organizational change, while Chapter 6 discusses how the process of planned change moves through the four levels. Chapter 7 describes a complex organizational change by using the levels construct. Chapter 8 shows how consultants and managers can intervene in the tasks and issues within each level. Chapter 9 concludes the book by integrating the key concepts.

Cases

To illustrate the discussion of levels we will present a series of cases. They are named below to help in their identification as we return to them at different points in our discussion. Some of the cases are large and some small; some are profit corporations and some not for profit. The authors have been consultants to each of the organizations.

The Head Ski case was complete before we met Howard Head, but consulting did take place with Howard Head while he was a participant in the Prince Company. These two cases are not disguised.

Transition University is a comprehensive private university with about 6000 students and programs in some seventy fields. The case spans two decades and two administrations.

Technical Institute is a research institute that is part of a large private research university. At any time it has about 100 faculty and a varied number of research programs.

Modular Building Company is part of a $400 million sales company that is publicly traded on the stock market. A leader in modular buildings and competitor of custom building manufacturers, the firm has been in business since the early 1900s.

Pharmaceutical Labs is a new entrepreneurial company that started with one over-the-counter product and has grown and diversified to a company of $100 million in sales and a significant product line of ethical drugs. The case spans ten years of the middle life of the company.

Universal Greeting Cards is a company that is privately held and has sales of about $800 million. It has diversified while trying to maintain excellence in its main business. The case covers a two-year period.

Religious Order is a large group of religious men that are part of an international group. They are involved in education at all levels and pastoral work in an international setting. The group in the case has about 500 members and the international group about 24,000. This case spans two decades.

Long Distance Communications Company (LCD) is part of an extensive communications company responsible for installation and maintenance of long distance communications circuits. The company is public and experiencing tremendous environmental change. The group in the case represents one major segment of the company and employs in excess of 10,000 workers.

Regional Blue Cross and Blue Shield is a large medical insurance company in the Blues system. It is a not-for-profit organization by its structure, and to keep this status it provides service to the medical needs of those who cannot afford to pay for all the care their high-risk medical conditions require. Yet it competes with for-profit insurance carriers in the medical field.

2

Organizational Levels: Theory and Practice

Conceptual Foundation

When thinking in terms of levels in organizations, we should not only distinguish between hierarchy/echelon and complexity, but focus on complexity as a more fruitful way to analyze organizational phenomena and organizational change processes. Levels of complexity—individual, group, intergroup, total organizational—are frequently used as frameworks for understanding organizational processes (Leavitt, 1979; Harrison, 1987). Several essential points need to be clarified about the concept and usage of the term *organizational levels*. The notion of level of complexity must be distinguished from that of echelon (Rousseau, 1985). Echelon refers to position on a chain of command in an organization, such as worker, supervisor, middle manager. Levels of organizational behavior, however, can be thought of as levels of complexity, as described, for instance, by Miller (1978) with regard to biological systems. This is a more fruitful way to analyze organizational phenomena and organizational change processes. Miller identifies seven levels of biological organization: cell, organ, organism, group, organization, society, and supernatural. They are hierarchical in that each system is composed of interrelated subsystems in a hierarchical order; that is, organs are composed of cells, organisms composed of organs, and so on. The hierarchical nature of the system also means that if any of its subsystems ceases to carry out its function, the system ceases to exist. Therefore, a dynamic notion of levels of complexity is needed to more fully understand, appreciate, and manage behavior in a complex organizational system. The subsystems that make up an organization as a social system are the individual, the face-to-face working team, the interdepartmental group of teams, and the organization.

Four Levels of Organizational Behavior

We are presenting levels in terms of how people participate in organizations. Moreover, we will discuss how linking the levels to one another provides an additional useful tool and core skills for managers, consultants, and teachers of organizational behavior (Coghlan and Rashford, 1991). This framework's four levels of participation—individual, face-to-face team, interdepartmental group, and organizational—can be viewed as degrees or types of involvement, subsystems, or degrees of complexity depending on one's perspective. From the point of view of the individual, there are different tasks that involve one at each level of organization (Table 2.1). From the point of view of management, the tasks at each level involve different modalities of participation in the organization (Table 2.2).

Each organizational level can be viewed from two perspectives—input and output. Input tends to be from the smaller system to the larger, while output is perceived from the larger system to the smaller. From the point of view of the individual, the least complex participation is the membership that the individual has in the organization in order to meet personal life goals (Level I). More complex participation is required in estab-

Table 2.1
Tasks at Each of the Four Organizational Levels from an Individual Perspective

Level	Task
I. Individual	Membership and participation
II. Face-to-face team	Creating effective working relationships
III. Interdepartmental group	Coordinating joint effort
IV. Organizational	Adapting

Table 2.2
Tasks at Each of the Four Organizational Levels from a Management Perspective

Level	Task
I. Individual	Involvement
II. Face-to-face team	Productive team functioning
III. Interdepartmental group	Coordination of effective output
IV. Organizational	Competitive advantage

lishing effective working relationships in a face-to-face team while maintaining personal integrity (Level II). An even more complex involvement exists in terms of the interdepartmental group or divisional type of interface, where teams must coordinate their efforts in order to achieve complex tasks and maintain a balance of power among competing political interest groups (Level III). Finally, the most complex, from the point of view of the individual, is the relationship of the total organization to its external environment, in which organizations compete for scarce resources to produce similar products or services. The key task for any organization is to adapt to environmental forces driving for change (Level IV).

From management's perspective (the output perspective in systems terms), the core issue is one of involvement. The most basic form of involvement is to establish good, working, face-to-face relationships in functional teams. The third level of involvement is the group or divisional level, in which complex information and data systems are used to extend the knowledge and to coordinate the functions of the total working group, made up of multiple face-to-face teams. Finally, the most complex of all is the unified effort of all participants in an organization toward the goal of making the organization profitable, growth-oriented, and functional in its external environment. This set of complex behaviors, then, is separated into a cognitive map—a mental construct of different types of participation and involvement—by the use of the concept of levels.

Both sides of the tasks at each level—the individual's and management's—are combined to describe the four tasks at each of the four organizational levels (Table 2.3). The four key tasks of *bonding, creating a functioning working team that is productive, coordination,* and *adaptation* form a complex pattern.

Within each level there are tasks. As seen from the tables, these tasks are double-sided. There is the task from viewpoint within each level, such as the individual's task to be an individual or the team's task to function well, and there is the task from the outside viewpoint at each level, such as management's requirement that an individual belong or that a team be effective. These dual tasks coexist at each level and create a tension between them. These tensions have been well described by Fox (1985). Within a unitary frame of reference, the tension is between individual and organizational goals, and its resolution comes through effective human resource management. Within a pluralist frame the tensions are between competing political self-interest groups, and the resolution is through bargaining and negotiation. Within the radical frame, the tension fundamentally cannot be resolved within the organizational context and so it is enacted on the wider stage of society and politics.

It is in the working out of these tensions and the completion of the relevant tasks that participation at each level is most successful. For example, on Level I, in a career interview, the manager must suppress the need to praise or rebuke productivity performance since the focus of such an interview is on how the individual can improve his or her own personal development and growth. For example, on Level II a team can work through its internal dynamics and create a cohesive, functioning unit, while at the same time, it meets the organization's demands to be effective in terms measured by others outside the team.

Table 2.3
Common Tasks at Each of the Four Organizational Levels

Level	Task
I. Individual	Bonding
II. Face-to-face team	Creating a functioning team
III. Interdepartmental group	Coordination
IV. Organizational	Adaptation

Within each level are behaviors that contribute to the successful completion of the level's tasks.

Interventions

The levels framework provides important insights into the types of intervention that are desirable in any OD program. Each level demands its own most appropriate or *key* intervention to help fulfill the primary task of that level and also suggests the most relevant interventions to help link the task of the levels to one another. In our view, some interventions are more useful than others in resolving the core issues that define each level. An OD consultant utilizes interventions according to the joint diagnosis by consultant and client as to what is needed in a given situation. Our notion of key intervention does not predetermine or limit a consultant's ability to intervene effectively in the concrete situation of any given consultation.

Level I: Individual

Individuals within organizations have life-tasks, needs, and wishes that extend far beyond their participation in any given work setting. Each individual struggles to find unique personal satisfaction in work as well. Management expects individuals to belong to the organization in an appropriate though unwritten psychological contract. When the tasks at this level are reasonably and adequately met, the organization and its goals can be a source of personal goal motivation. People will retain their individuality while "belonging" to the organization. In contrast, the awareness and utilization of motivational techniques are the basic functions management uses to enhance the growth and effectiveness of each member of the organization. Management's ideal goal is to create a matching process that benefits individuals and the organization. Enabling and encouraging individuals to be involved results in their finding that the work situation develops them as human beings while benefiting the organization (Schein, 1978). Individuals do not always relate to management's goal in this regard, however, and many prefer to define the relationship with the organization in political and adversarial teams around issues of power and control (Fox, 1985).

Inevitably, tension arises from this matching process (Argyris, 1990a; Schein, 1978). Individuals attempt to be themselves and bring their unique aspects to the organization while adapting to organizational norms. One common difficulty in managing people is that the plurality of views and applied theories of how to motivate people produce contradictory approaches and undermine the growth process (McGregor, 1960; Schein, 1980). The manager who thinks that motivation is external and must be applied by force is in sharp contrast to the manager or subordinate who thinks that motivation comes from within the person. The tension becomes even more critical if in unexamined behavior a manager proposes one point of view but acts on the other. Managers need to reflect on how to motivate different people in different and changing circumstances. The more ownership and awareness individuals have of their lives, the more capable they are of contributing their unique qualities and skills, which are so necessary for organizations to change and develop.

The key intervention on this level is the *career interview,* in which the dynamics of the life cycle, the work cycle, and the family cycle are examined and juxtaposed conceptually to enable the individual to locate his or her career in the context of his or her life (Schein, 1978). The person-centered nature of the interview encourages the individual to take ownership of his or her life and career and adopt positive coping responses to the tasks he or she faces. The career interview can empower individuals to initiate and promote change in the organization. At the same time, managers can utilize the process to reflect on and restructure managerial assumptions and behavior. A technique such as the career anchor exercise, based on the individual's work experience, needs, and values, is of great significance (Schein, 1990). In the career anchor, that aspect of work which produces a sense of identity and self-concept in work is located by the individual and can be used to establish a contract with the organization about the individual's contribution to the corporate endeavor and the organization's response.

CASE: An electrical engineer at Long Distance Communications Company (LDC) was promoted to a managerial position. After some time in the job, he reported to his superior that he was unhappy in this role and that he would prefer to return to the technical area of product design, where he felt at home in the field of technological research. Because his superior knew and understood him, this request was granted. This recognition by the superior that the engineer's career anchor was technical functional, rather than managerial, enabled the organization and the individual to reconfigure the relationship between them so as to achieve a better match of the individual's desires, skills, and motivations with the organization's needs.

Labor unions deserve a note of their own with regard to Level I. Union members experience Level I bonding to two organizations at the same time: the union and the firm that employs them. Training, skill development, and grievance protection are offered by the union. Promotion to a supervisory position is like moving from one organization to another. Management may have to allow for a plan of return to the assembly line to persuade a union member to accept a supervisory position. The individual may sacrifice self-esteem and bonding with other union members by entering a new relationship and bonding with management. Like the engineer in the previous example, the person may need to know a return path exists.

Level I applies throughout an organization, but it works differently at different points in the chain of command. A secretary's or worker's commitment to the organization differs from that of the CEO. Level I dysfunction involving a member of top management has different consequences from dysfunction involving a warehouse clerk. If the dysfunction emanates from management policy, the effects can vary throughout the organization. By Level I dysfunction is meant that because of assumption, attitudes, or behaviors of either the individual or the organization's management, the Level I task of bonding is frustrated with consequential negative results for working relationships, interteam cooperation, and ultimately the functioning of the organization.

CASE: At Long Distance Communications (LDC) the manager of design engineering had a serious drinking problem. His behavior was blocking communications to that whole area of the organization; projects were running into difficulty. Top management was afraid to confront the man because of his long association with the firm. His problems were disguised because the group was working on organizational problems. The managers involved had not acknowledged that an individual's alcoholism was at the root of the problem and felt they should be able to solve the problem. The consultant intervened to tease out what was going on by mirroring the individual's behavior to the group and questioning whether this behavior was related to the organization's problem-solving. As people began to realize that there was no correlation between the behavior and project, senior management became convinced that there was indeed an issue outside the workplace and the individual in question was sent to an alcohol counselor for evaluation. After treatment and with the support of the group, the individual was able to resume functioning in the workplace, and the issues subsequently resolved themselves. Long Distance Communications will be visited again in our case of complex change.

CASE: In a case not unlike the Head Ski Company, the founder of Pharmaceutical Labs was the chief operating officer. Having begun his career in sales, he viewed the staff as if they were sales persons and only rewarded the sales function. He did not recognize the contribution that other functions made to the organization. His own total dedication to sales, increasing sales, and personal goal-setting made him blind to the contribution of any other function as his firm grew. What he relished was the ability to make the sale. When a career interview helped him realize this, the founder-entrepreneur agreed to move into the role of chairman and appointed another person as president to manage the company. More than any other intervention, the career interview produces a sense of bonding and affirms personal growth.

Level II: Face-to-Face Team

From the individual's perspective, entry into the work activity involves interfacing with other individuals in clearly defined units. Face-to-face teams are typically formal groups and defined by

1. Face-to-face interaction
2. Common objectives
3. Psychological awareness of other members, and
4. Self-definition as a team, with member/nonmember boundaries clearly defined

Level II is more complex than Level I because of the increased number of participants and interactions. Teams form part of a wider system in organizations, and some of the problems that arise within the team may originate beyond the team in its technological and political interface with other teams. Conflicts that arise between teams are considered at Level III.

From the managerial perspective, any individual's task within the face-to-face team is to contribute to the collective ventures of the team. Management requires the team to be efficient and cooperative in delivering its output toward the overall organizational tasks. Effective team functioning requires the team to succeed in accomplishing its tasks and learn from its experience in building and maintaining working relationships.

The team's process, then, focuses on becoming a functioning work unit that builds on success and learns from mistakes. It is critical for face-to-face teams to develop techniques and skills of self-reflection in order to correct their own dysfunctions. Such skills define successful teams. Level II dysfunctions occur when assumptions, attitudes, and behavior of team members toward one another and toward the team's effort frustrate the team's performance. Generally the discovery of negative information tends to be not valued in organizations because people then tend to confront one another. This results from the learned patterns of inference, attribution, and the placing of blame. Behaviors such as blaming, withholding information, inappropriate team leader style, misplaced competition, sexism and racism, and lack of trust can detract from the team members' capacity to work well together. Furthermore, within any given team the interaction skills of task achievement and maintenance function may not be equally developed. In most organizations, performance is not measured on the team level but on the individual level. Subsequently, rewards may be divisive in teams, they may break up teams through the transfer of successful individual members, or, conversely, sanctions may impose restrictive norms and practices. The team dynamics described above are relevant to all teams, whether in top management or middle management or in worker-maintenance areas in an organization.

The key intervention on the face-to-face team level consists in formally building up team skills. Team-building is the title given to a wide range of activities aimed at improving a work team's effectiveness. Team skills comprise four activities in descending order of importance (Beckhard, 1972; Kolb, Rubin, and McIntyre, 1984):

1. Setting goals and priorities
2. Analyzing and allocating work
3. Examining the team's process, and
4. Examining the interpersonal relationships among team members

Team-building is the key intervention because it deals with members' participation, the team's goals and work allocation, and ways to increase the team's productivity (Reddy and Jamison, 1988). Other interventions focus on less comprehensive issues and provide team process skills in communication, problem-solving, decision-making, member roles and functions, cultural rules of interaction, norm evaluation, conflict management, leadership style and the exercise of influence, and initiating and managing change (Schein, 1988). Team development provides a framework for understanding the growth stages of the collective personality that is the team and, through cultural analysis, for uncovering the hidden assumptions that constitute the team's relationship to its internal and external environment (Schein, 1992).

CASE: A committee established by a bishop to create a pastoral plan for the diocese invited David Coghlan to work with its members because it was experiencing severe interpersonal difficulties. Meetings were proving to be stressful; members frequently felt hurt by each others' comments and several were reported to be on the verge of resigning. After being briefed by a delegation from the committee, the consultant designed a process for a two-day meeting. At the outset he invited each member to write down what he or she thought were the committee's mission and purpose. He did this in order to ground any later treatment of interpersonal relations in the committee's reason for existence, the way it structured its tasks, and the way its process worked. When the members shared their perceptions of the committee's mission and purpose, both the consultant and the committee noticed that there were practically as many versions of the mission as there were members, and that many of the perceptions were incompatible. It emerged that the purpose of the committee had changed since it was originally established, and that some members were working from a new definition, some from the original one, and others from variations on both. The two-day meeting was then devoted to clarifying and articulating a common purpose for the committee and its work. Very little time was subsequently given to the topic of interpersonal relations. The consultant, in presenting the team-building model outlined above, pointed out that if the goals and mission of the committee had remained unclarified and in dispute, then any work on interpersonal relations within the team would at best be temporary and the problems would resurface. Subsequent reports from the committee indicated that interpersonal relations among the members did improve as the committee launched into its work with a clearer and agreed statement of purpose.

CASE: At Transition University the top management team found it difficult to adjust to the style of a new president, who encouraged open information-sharing and decision-making by consensus. His predecessor's approach had emphasized dividing up the work among subordinates and requiring them to focus on their own areas, do it themselves, and ignore others. The predecessor's way of doing things had been in place for almost ten years and was replicated in the behavior of his subordinates. The new president's style and approach were in distinct contradiction to these long-established and habitual behavioral patterns. Most observers at the university had the reaction that the new president's style would not last long, that it was a passing fad, and that it was he who should adapt to the organizational norms, since they were in place and were part of the university's tradition. It was only when some of the benefits of the new approach began to become apparent—and making them apparent was a long process—that behavioral patterns began to change. Thereafter, the new president acted as a facilitator throughout the year, employing the services of a process consultant only at the start of each year. The president acted as a participant-consultant and participant-observer of the process and provided feedback on both process and content.

Level III: Interdepartmental Group

From the team's point of view, to be effective and enter the organization's life is to work within a larger system. Level III is made up of any number of face-to-face working teams that must function together to accomplish a divisional purpose, such as manufacturing, sales, or marketing, or it is a collection of individual work teams that provide a strategic business unit function for an organization. The *interdepartmental group level* needs to

1. Have the ability to sense critical information
2. Pass beyond the barriers of individual teams in order to implement programs through coordination, and
3. Project at a range beyond their direct contact—that is, deal with people not in their immediate group team or functional department

In large organizations where size and distance dissolve immediate personal relationships, it is imperative that this level function well. From management's view, the team's task within the group is to perform as a team while having a sense of belonging to the group from which it receives the scarce resources enabling it to function. When this third level is working effectively, the group or division is capable of obtaining information and applying it in decision-making for the implementation of complex programs or operations. The task of this level is to map the flow of information and partially completed work from one unit to another. Top management requires that these units form a coordinated aggregate. Performing a complex function and distributing scarce resources, such as personnel and money appropriately, is the key venture at the group level. In this highly political situation the inherent structural conflicts of multiple interest-groups or parties need to be resolved. This diversified collection of differing functions and interests must, as a group, negotiate an outcome that reflects the balance of power among competing coalitions and distributes resources justly. An essential element in Level III dynamics centers on issues of power and the way it is exercised in the allocation of resources and information.

From management's view, the technical issues at this level require an ability to locate dysfunctions. Dysfunctions occur in the flow of information and partially completed work or services from one team to another. The entire function must be viewed, understood, and successfully handled in order to produce the product or service. Because of a huge number of individuals engaged in particular functions in a large organization, this entire function is often very difficult to see. The interdepartmental group's task is to become a functioning work unit by building on successes and learning from mistakes. Difficulties also arise at this level because of insufficient reflective and corrective skills. Discovery of negative information is difficult because it is often hidden in the interfaces between teams. The organizational rewards system often does not reflect the actual needs of particular functioning units within the larger group.

The key intervention on the interdepartmental group level consists of internal mapping. Individual heads of work units or team leaders are asked to plot the work flow through their section from start to finish, showing all the intermediate links between functioning teams. All members of the group then have a chance to jointly own the dysfunctional areas and work in small task forces to address the dysfunctions. This process, first referred to by Dick Beckhard in some unpublished notes, is a simple one requiring each manager to list each input and output from his or her own area on a large sheet of newsprint. At an interdepartmental group meeting these sheets are taped together and the quality and effectiveness of each point of connection between teams are evaluated. The process for correcting dysfunction is to set a marker or flag at each point of dysfunction and assemble a task force of affected individuals to correct the dysfunction. Most often the dysfunction is *between* working teams and not in them.

Severe dysfunctions on an interdepartmental group level are most often solved through the use of a consultant who can help the group configure its information and its materials handling processes, and restructure itself, if necessary to a new configuration. Knowledge of content is essential. A consultant must be conversant with the content of the technology in an information flow or decision-making process. Other interventions utilize Program Evaluation and Review Technique (PERT) and Critical Path Method (CPM) techniques to map complex work flow patterns and timing.

CASE: Providing an example of this intervention is Modular Building Company, a manufacturer of modular factory/warehouse units that competes with manufacturers of stand-alone units uniquely suited to each operation. The company's problem was that deliveries were not being made on time. Accordingly, a consultant was hired who gathered the heads of major departments and facilitated a detailed mapping of each step in the process of manufacturing the modules, making adaptations to fit customers' requirements, and delivering the product, from input to output. Time delays and the reasons for them were identified. Inadequacies in meeting other departments' needs, the points of dissension or conflict between the departmental areas, were carefully worked out. After some thoughtful reflection it became apparent that while there were unique requirements for each customer, there were also many common elements. If Sales sat down with Engineering to define a customer's needs, often predesigned engineering solutions were available that could fit the customer's needs without requiring extremely time-consuming custom engineering. As a result of this intervention's mapping, the time it took to build modified units dropped significantly.

CASE: Level III interdepartmental group dysfunction does not necessarily take place only within the work flow, but it often takes place within the resource flow. For example, at Technical Institute a major research unit of a large university was functioning as a research unit within one of the university's schools. The dean of the school had appointed an associate dean as head of finance. The associate dean's function was to make sure that the expenditure of funds matched the university's needs and requirements. The individual had good financial skills for managing the resources of the university. The faculty of Technical Institute, on the other hand, wanted flexibility in dealing with academic and research matters and wanted a quick response for access to the financial resources that the institution was garnering from outside sources. They directed a great deal of frustration and anger at the associate dean because of his failure to understand the dynamics of the group when insisting on financial accuracy concerning their use of research funds and for requiring that they find matching funding, as other institutes and some regular departments required. Intervention in this situation, rather than an internal mapping process, focused on helping the research group to articulate its needs for support from the financial function of the dean's office while encouraging the group to listen to the dean's explanation of the need for common reporting practices across the institute.

Level IV: Organizational

The fourth level of complexity in an organization concerns the organization's goals, policy, or strategy. It is the fusion of the three other levels to form a working, cohesive organization that interacts in its own semiclosed system or environment. The organization's task is

1. To be cohesive
2. To live in a competitive environment
3. To exchange a product or service to obtain scarce resources
4. To reflect on its own strengths and weaknesses, and
5. To engage in a proactive relationship to determine the opportunities and threats from the external environment

Strengths and opportunities are matched in a selection process that determines programs, services, and products aimed at accomplishing the goals of the organization and serving the external environment. An awareness of the cultural assumptions that underlie an organization's policies, strategies, structures, and behaviors contributes to successful completion of the tasks at this level (Schein, 1992).

The key intervention is open systems planning, performed in terms of the organization's core mission, with the internal and external constituencies that make demands on the organization (Freeman, 1984). Open systems planning entails identifying key stakeholders in the environment and (1) analyzing the demands they are currently making on the organization, (2) projecting demands they will make, (3) determining the current responses to those demands, and (4) creating a plan of action to create a desired future (Beckhard and Harris, 1987; Beckhard and Pritchard, 1992; Coghlan, 1990a).

One of the most critical stages in the open systems planning process is clarifying a series of points between the present state and the desired future state. Organizations often make the mistake of attempting to go directly from the present state to the future state. This traumatic and often too extensive change fails and brings the whole change process to a halt. Managers and the consultants they employ must detail and plot intermediate steps on a course of incremental change from the present to the desired future state.

CASE: Pharmaceutical Labs was a company that began by manufacturing a single product, a calcium dietary supplement. As the product gained popularity with consumers and the operation grew, the firm began a conscious program of acquisitions. A company that manufactured a chair lift for stairs and one that made eyeglasses were purchased. These organizational components would generally be classified in the medical or health field. A period of significant growth was followed by a flat period in which the company found this wide range of activities difficult to manage. The president called a key management team into his office to discern the company's core mission. They decided the company should become a manufacturer of ethical pharmaceuticals (prescription drugs), and they began a systematic placement of the firm in that business. The first approach was to encourage the development of new ethical products by the research and development department. The period from the initiation of basic research to production of a marketable product in this field is long, however, at least fourteen years. Therefore the key team came up with a second strategy: to acquire from abroad other products that could be manufactured and sold in the United States under license. This process produced a marketable product in three years. The dual strategy combining research and development and product licensing was used systematically to shape the organization from within and simultaneously develop strategic advantage in the market. The firm placed itself in a particular competitive marketplace while developing a strong market position with strong new products.

In developing its core mission, Pharmaceutical Labs found out it could not sustain being a medical company. A medical company was too broad and had too many supply channels and marketplaces on which to focus as a single organization. Second, it realized that its original main product was sold over the counter through pharmacies and that this, in turn, was a different market from the ethical drugs prescribed by physicians and sold in pharmacies under prescription. Both these insights contributed to the refinement of the firm's core mission. The company decided that the most lucrative market was the specialized ethical drugs sold through pharmacies under physicians' prescriptions. The result of this decision was that the other product lines no longer consistent with the company's mission were sold off, and the funds from their sale were used to obtain the rights to products that would be within the pharmaceutical specialty. The firm realized that the research and testing needed to obtain U.S. Food and Drug Administration (FDA) certification that a drug is safe for use is so lengthy that it would not be possible to make up ground quickly on competitors. The average ten or more years of basic research and ten years of testing mean that many new products do not reach the market until fifteen or twenty years after inception. Careful discussion and thought-provoking focus enabled the company to decide to purchase the rights to drugs already in the testing process in foreign countries, and so reduce the "catch-up" time to four or five years.

The strategy of using foreign drugs is a good example of incremental change, establishing an interim state between the present and future states. When management defined its new niche, the ability to start from scratch and create new ethical drugs was still a distant dream. An intermediate point, but moving in that direction, was to take drugs already in existence, with some original testing of their efficacy and safety already done, and bring them into the marketplace more quickly by completing the testing required by the FDA. This alternative shortened the time required to meet its goal and gave the pharmaceutical company an intermediate life.

The "Key" Individual, Team, Group/Division, and Organization

We have made the critical distinction between organizational levels and echelon and pointed out that they are not the same although there is a strong connection. Positioning on an organization's hierarchy has an impact on functioning or dysfunction. When someone has a problem, the higher that individual is in the echelon, the greater the impact of the problem on the organization. We saw how Howard Head's individual Level I issue soon became a Level IV issue. The higher one is in the echelon or the more power a team has, the greater the influence is to bring about change. The problem of an interdepartmental group or divisional leader is more than a Level II issue for his or her team. The charismatic founder-entrepreneur is legendary in having an impact on an organization's life, style, and functioning.

To develop that idea further we refer to the notion of the *key* individual, the person who by virtue of power, position, charisma, or expertise influences outcomes more than other individuals can. Similarly within organizations, there is the notion of the key team and the key group. In engineering organizations, the lead engineering group may be the key group. In manufacturing organizations, over different stages of the life cycle the key group may shift from design engineering to production to sales. In universities there is typically competition among academic departments, administration, and finance as to which is the key group. In competitive markets where organizations compete for clients and customers, there are key organizations; they are preeminent, the market leaders from which other organizations tend to position themselves. In organization development, process interventions must be owned in the organization from the top. If an intervention is to be successful, the issues around key individuals must be understood and dealt with first (Greiner and Schein, 1988; Kakabadse and Parker, 1984).

Summary

In this chapter we have discussed organizational membership through the notion of the four levels of behavior and distinguished it from echelon or hierarchy. We have also outlined the organizational processes that take place at each level. These processes are characterized by a key word that defines the essence of each level: for Level I, *bonding;* for Level II, *functioning team;* for Level III, *coordination;* and for Level IV, *adaptation* (Table 2.3). Finally we have noted that within the issues of each level there is a twin focus: actions that enable completion of the relevant tasks of the level and actions that facilitate significant interrelationships between levels. These actions will be explained further in Chapters 3 and 4.

The construct of four organizational levels of complexity is essential for understanding the dynamic interrelationships among individuals, teams, aggregations of teams, and an organization's strategic endeavors. It integrates the disciplines of individual and group psychology with those of strategic management, technology, and industrial relations. In our view, it is located at the cutting edge of organization development and the management of change.

3

Defining the Space Within the Four Organizational Levels

In the previous chapters we looked at the four levels primarily in terms of membership, outlined some of the processes that take place at each level, and described how the four levels are linked to one another. This chapter goes into further detail on the content and process of each level and demonstrates what the consultant or manager can observe and how to work within the levels framework.

The concept of *process* is essential to understand how to work with individuals, teams, interdepartmental groups, and organizations. "Process" refers to *how* things are done, whereas "content" refers to *what* is done. What should a consultant or manager focus on when trying to work in a situation in order to improve it? Edgar Schein, in his *Process Consultation, Volume 2* (1987), distinguishes between task and interpersonal issues in terms of content, process, and structure in a six-cell framework. *Task content* refers to what the organization, interdepartmental group, team, or individual is intending to do: its mission, the task to be done, the problems arising around clarity of mission, assignment of functions to meet tasks, and analysis of information. A consultant's or manager's key role is to keep the client system (organization, interdepartmental group, team, individual) focused on what it is doing.

Task process refers to how the organization, interdepartmental group, team, or individual engage in defining mission, setting goals, completing tasks, reviewing progress, and so on. These issues require attention if the tasks are to be completed satisfactorily. The consultant pays attention to how the issues of task are dealt with and intervenes to help the organization, interdepartmental group, team, or individual manage its process. *Task structure* refers to the basic assumptions that have formed around critical task issues. These sets of assumptions constitute the organization's "culture" (Schein, 1992). They become embedded in the organization and in the teams and interdepartmental groups that make up the organization. These assumptions eventually come to be taken for granted and accordingly disappear from consciousness. Passed on to new members implicitly, they become in effect a structured way of thinking and behaving. Because they pertain to the organization's survival in the external environment, they focus on the issues of mission, goal setting, task accomplishment, and problem solving.

Interpersonal content refers to the particular roles members of an organization play with regard to other members: supporting, interrupting, ignoring, controlling, manipulating, and attacking. *Interpersonal process,* which overlaps somewhat with interpersonal content, focuses more on what is happening in the team, interdepartmental group, or organization, and how they function in relation to the members: how people listen or don't listen to each other, how they agree or disagree over specific issues, and how they support each other or support some people more than others. *Interpersonal structure* refers to how authority and peer relationships are defined, how thoughts and feelings are expressed, how influence is exercised, and how crises are dealt with.

We have found Schein's framework useful and practical in our teaching and consulting work. We have developed it to include the issues of each of the four organizational levels, so that the consultants or managers can focus their observations and interventions in order to facilitate the successful completion of the tasks of each of the four levels. "Interpersonal" in Schein's framework becomes "relational." In systemic thinking, the *interpersonal* tends to be interpreted as referring to relations between individuals, while *relational* comprises intercollective relationships.

Foci of Observation and Intervention on Four Levels

Level I: The Individual

The central task at Level I is to achieve and to maintain appropriate *bonding* between the individual and the organization. Table 3.1 outlines the core issues with regard to task, process, and structure at this level.

Task Content   The task content is the actual job to be done, and for the individual, the role in the organization by which he or she is expected to do that job. Task content on Level I centers on the psychological contract between individual and organization. The contract is reciprocal, specifying both the individual's growth and developmental needs and the productivity to be returned to the organization. A consultant may work with a manager on issues such as job description, role clarity, achievements of targets, management by objectives (MBO), problem-analysis, and the integration of job description with organizational needs.

Task Process   Within an organization the main task process is the performance review, which assesses the individual's degree of success in achieving goals set previously. The con-

Table 3.1
Focus of Observation and Intervention on Level I

	Task	**Relational**
Content	Job description Role description and goal-setting	Career path Career anchor
Process	Performance review Job design	Career interview
Structure	Managerial assumptions about work and work motivation	Assumptions about organizations and individual skills
Outcome	*Bonding*	

sultant may work with the manager on how to go about attaining and fostering others' attainment of goals. This could include analyzing issues such as the effect of executive work stations and information technology on the manager's job and time management, and the best way to conduct a performance review.

Task Structure   The task structure refers to the managerial assumptions that govern assessment of the individual's work. McGregor (1960) and Schein (1980) have demonstrated that restrictive managerial assumptions about human nature in relation to work tend to be self-limiting, a self-sealing prophecy actualized in behavioral strategies that limits outcome. By challenging a manager's assumptions about work motivation, a consultant may enable him or her to recognize the limitations of the attitudes that underlie behavioral action.

Relational Content   The relational content is the individual's career path in the organization and the individual's particular "anchor" (Schein, 1990). Schein points to eight possible career anchors that emerge from an individual's perception of his or her own competence, motives, and values; the individual's anchor may be technical-functional competence, general managerial competence, autonomy or independence, security/stability, entrepreneurial creativity, service or dedication to a cause, pure challenge, and life style. A consultant or manager can help the individual understand and assess his or her own career anchor.

Relational content also includes an open contract renewable as growth occurs. While the person's anchor is stable and does not change, application of the anchor and personal skills will change over time as one progresses in a career. In a similar way, organizational needs change and require different applications of individual skills. The consultant may promote inquiry and dialogue between individuals and management so they can explore possibilities of a reconfigured match in such changing circumstances.

Relational Process   The relational process is the career interview, whereby the individual's life cycle, work cycle, and family cycle are located and placed in juxtaposition so that the individual can situate his or her career in the context of his or her life (Schein, 1978, 1990). It is critical to avoid mixing the performance review with a career interview. Understanding the patterns of the life cycle can enable a manager to realize that people can and do change, and that needs change over time. The honest manager may have to encourage movement out of the organization in order to enable the individual to grow. It is not uncommon for an organization to be incapable of accepting people who, through acquired educational growth, desire to take on different roles or more responsibility in an organization. The consultant may assist a manager to make such an assessment and promote dialogue in this subject among his staff.

Relational Structure The relational structure refers to how the underlying career anchor colors the individual's perceptions of life in the organization and reflects the individual's part of the psychological contract. An individual whose career anchor is technical-functional may approach all relationships and organizational processes from an engineering perspective and assume, for example, that all problems can be solved rationally. Different people have different interests and skills and can continue to be desirable to the organization if the organization can adapt to these different interests. The point that one occupies in a life cycle or due to conditions from outside or family interests may cause these interests to diminish or change. The consultant may confront the manager on how his or her career anchor colors perception of how the organization should function and may assist inquiry into the perceptions of other work colleagues.

Level II: The Face-to-Face Team

The task at Level II is to create a *functioning team that is productive*. Table 3.2 outlines the content, process, and structure issues on this level.

Task Content The team's mission, goals, achievement of those goals in measurable terms and the work done is its task content. The consultant inquires into how clear the goals are, what measure of ownership surrounds them in the team, which tasks need to be done to achieve the goals, and how achievement can be measured.

Table 3.2
Focus of Observation and Intervention on Level II

	Task	**Relational**
Content	Set and achieve team goals	How members work together
Process	Allocate work to team members	Team processes
Structure	Standard operating procedures	Recurrent interpersonal relationships and roles
Outcome	**_Creating a Functioning Team That is Productive_**	

Task Process   Understanding the task process requires discovering how the work is allocated to achieve goals, by whom and how that is decided, how the work is done, how progress is reviewed, and how dysfunctions are identified and corrected. By observing the team at work, the consultant can assist the team to stand back from its activity and examine its own process (Schein, 1988).

Task Structure   The task structure of the team is the standard operating procedure whereby the team goes about its work. Informal standard operating procedures can be very powerful. Team members may be quite unaware of the effects of informal procedures. As an outsider, a consultant can observe the behavioral effects of these procedures and facilitate the team's uncovering the assumptions that underlie their existence and operation.

Relational Content   The team members' work with one another is the relational content of Level II. Belbin (1981) identifies the following roles, which he judges to be essential if the team is to be effective: specialist, completer, implementor, teamworker, monitor, evaluator, shaper, coordinator, resource investigator, and the plant. Some of these roles emphasize the creation of vision in the team's work, others focus on task accomplishment, while others attend to team issues. Each of these roles plays a key part in enabling a team to deal with complex issues. A consultant can help the members of a team identify the composite strengths of the mix of personality types and orientations in the team and feel less anxious in working together in the face of different styles or an imbalance of styles.

Relational Process The relational process is the way the team solves problems, makes decisions, handles conflict, exercises leadership. By observing the team at work, a consultant can help a team learn from its experiences of process, particularly if different processes occur when the task content is going well or doing poorly (Schein, 1988).

Relational Structure In the relational structure of the team, interpersonal roles become recurrent: how some individuals are consistently ignored or have less status, women are treated differently from men, and so on. Although the effects of these structures may be readily apparent to the consultant as an outsider, it is important that the consultant be ultrasensitive in this area so as to ensure that individual members of the team are not exposed and humiliated in front of their colleagues and that any member saves face in an examination of his or her position in the team (Schein, 1987).

Level III: The Interdepartmental Group

The task at Level III is the *coordination* of the resources and interaction of multiple teams. Table 3.3 outlines the issues of content, process, and structure at this level.

Task Content The task content is the basic differentiation within the organization of function, structure, and the allocation of resources to each function. It includes the allocation of information and the structure of information services, which may in themselves define organizational differentiation. Differentiation can be based on function, geography, project, line. A consultant or manager can work with the interdepartmental group to clarify and make changes in the structure of an organization.

Table 3.3
Focus of Observation and Intervention on Level III

	Task	**Relational**
Content	Division of organizational functions Division of resources Structure of MIS	Resource exchange Quality of information Timely information Collective bargaining outcomes
Process	Determination of compatibility Determination of input/output Application of specialties or professional field to the organization	Decision support systems PERT, internal mapping Allocation of resources to fit input/output Collective bargaining
Structure	Assumptions and sharing of information and resources	Subcultures
Outcome	*Coordination*	

Task Process   Level III task process pertains to each function's compatibility with the overall organizational mission, goals, and tasks, and to resource allocation on that basis. The consultant can work with the interdepartmental group on how each unit receives its resources, how the work flows, how teams interrelate, how information is passed from one unit to another so that the output by one unit matches the input of another. Engineering or computer specialties are applied to the organization at this level.

Task Structure   Organizations develop basic assumptions about the different functions within an organization's structure. An example is the assumption that the informal status of a particular structure cannot be changed: for instance, that finance is only a service and is not critical, that engineering is more important than production, and so forth. A consultant would help management uncover and confront such assumptions. These assumptions can change over time. Engineering is key in new product development, whereas marketing is key in older product lines.

Relational Content The relational content of Level III is flow of information or work—the management information system (MIS) and the quality and timeliness of information as it flows from one unit to another at this interdepartmental group level. Another element in this area is the balance of power between coalitions as negotiated, for instance, in wage and salary agreements arrived at by collective bargaining.

Relational Process The process by which information flows through an organization and through decision support systems and such techniques as PERT and CPM is relational. It includes complex interteam relations, interteam conflict, processes of negotiation and collective bargaining, and internal mapping to solve cross-functional problems. The consultant can facilitate internal mapping, improve interteam relations, resolve conflict, and mediate in negotiations.

Relational Structure Organizations typically comprise a number of subcultures—workers, management, specialized departments or sections—who perceive themselves and others very differently than others do. The origins of these self-perceptions may be buried in the organization's history. In order to assist achievement of the coordination tasks, the consultant may help the interdepartmental group uncover assumptions about their component team and other teams that block effective coordination.

Level IV: The Organizational Level

The central task of Level IV is make the organization adapt to its external environment and thus survive. Table 3.4 outlines the content, process, and structural issues at this level.

Task Content The task content at the organizational level is survival. Through its strategic plan to achieve its mission, the organization maintains its position in profitability or providing a service. Accompanying success in this area is a sense of organizational worth. Consultants and strategic planners

Table 3.4
Focus of Observation and Intervention on Level IV

	Task	**Relational**
Content	Survival and profitability Attainment of mission Sense of organizational worth Total equity or endowment of the organization	Competitive advantage Stakeholder service Market share Perceived equity
Process	Open systems planning Strategic planning and management	Organizational adaptive coping cycle Management of change Organizational learning
Structure	Organizational self-image	Organizational environmental image
Outcome	*Adaptation*	

focus on content, particularly the choice of the right markets. Task content is often measured by the equity value of a firm, or in the case of a not-for-profit organization by the amount of the endowment.

Task Process   Typical processes whereby the organization's mission is achieved and its position maintained are open systems planning and management. Other more specific methodologies such as portfolio analysis, market share, and product life cycles may be utilized (Hax and Majluf, 1991).

Task Structure   The organization's self-image about its mission and possible contribution creates a confidence or diffidence in the organization's task performance. It determines the risks taken or not taken. A consultant may work with teams from top management, marketing, and sales to facilitate a change in self-image.

Relational Content   The relational content pertains to the relationship between an organization and its stakeholders, and between an organization and its competition. Stakeholder awareness and competitive strategy are essential elements (Freeman, 1984; Porter, 1980). The perceived value of an organization's stock or its market share or strength becomes a key element in the relational content on Level IV. The consultant may facilitate an open systems planning process whereby stakeholders and market demands are identified and strategies created to meet them.

Relational Process   The key relational process is to cope with a changing external environment by taking in pertinent information, transmitting it to the relevant sections of the organization, adapting production or services to meet the demands of the information, exporting an altered product or service, and receiving feedback from the environment as to the acceptability of the change (Schein, 1980). Internally this requires a process of change management and of dealing with the stages of denial, dodging, doing, and sustaining. This is the core of organization development and the work of OD consultants and will be developed further in Chapters 5 and 6.

Relational Structure   Basic assumptions about the organization in relation to its stakeholders and competitors, its self-image, and its potential for success can have a powerful impact on the creation of strategy and an organization's actual performance. A consultant may work with teams from top management, marketing, and sales to facilitate a change in self-image.

CASE: Regional Blue Cross and Blue Shield, a large midwestern regional health insurance organization, was structured functionally into two major segments: the hospital insurance side, which paid hospital bills, and the physicians' insurance side, which paid physician and outpatient bills. The organization was set up by operational functions. There were sales to individual customers, and there were sales to groups whose entire membership would be insured. The claims function processed subscribers' claims against insurance. The payment function made payments to hospitals and physicians. A follow-up group of service personnel was called Client Service. Away from the direct client aspects of the organization was Finance and Audit, a group that invested the monies from insurance payees so that these funds could earn money to be used in the payment of claims, and who also provided a financial audit of the whole operation and how it was functioning.

The external environment of the health insurance organization changed. The health maintenance organization (HMO) came into existence. An HMO is a group of physicians united under a particular insurance company, or it is a particular payer functioning as a group to review the patients and their needs in order to control costs by determining the appropriate way to tender medical services. Groups of physicians in a combined practice called a *physician provider organization* (PPO) also came into being. Such groups of physicians from different medical specialties operated together collectively by referring patients to one another for treatment and by providing services from the group at a reduced rate. The traditional payers also were funneled through the existing organization, and an additional block of business was brought into the insurance company from national accounts. While a large account, such as General Motors, was sold nationwide, operation of the plan was local—that is, a General Motors plant was located in a region.

The radical shift into a more complex and competitive business environment brought about a strategic plan within the company to change the structure of the organization. Each functioning unit—individual sales, group sales, claims, payment client services—was divided so that they would serve the HMO or the PPO or the individual sales or group sales area. This meant that throughout the organization the former claims group was split up, and the people needed to address these different areas were reassigned to functional areas by market segment. This process took over four months to accomplish; the planning had taken a year. It was led by the CEO, who felt that this change was critically important for the future of the organization. The major rationale was to have a competitive market-driven organization. The Level IV relational content issues of the change in the competitive market drove this change process. Yet the issues generated by this change must be examined in terms of four levels.

The most basic change on the individual level was that many people within the company felt that the structure of organization had changed dramatically. They had joined an organization that had operated within a bureaucratic framework, with promotions granted on the basis of grade and years of service. This now shifted to an entrepreneurial, competitive mode in which promotions and pay raises were no longer based on length of service, but rather on performance and productivity. On the team level, the new teams that were set up were no longer teams within the same function. There was no homogeneous work team within sales or within claims; instead, the new face-to-face teams were composed of people who were involved in sales, claims payment, and client services. This necessitated developing new terminology and more interactive work with people who had come from a different background and skill base.

The interdepartmental group level shift was the most dramatic. In the past, teams had been united by a single function. In the new structure, the teams were formed around the type of service delivered to the customer. This structure necessitated resource sharing within each of the functional areas in order to achieve efficiency in handling the new types of business. The shift meant that now the teams were in competition with each other. Each team competed with the other teams and paralleled their functions in trying to secure a profit for the organization. Clients could be moved from the HMO to the PPO or to group sales. As a consequence, the customer was affecting the success within each of the teams.

It was difficult to take the complex change processes that had occurred in this organization and explain them to the people involved in the change without the framework of the four organizational levels. Some people did not survive in the organization. Those who were happiest in the bureaucratic situation, where everything was functionally aligned, were very uncomfortable in the competitive situation, where the focus was on customer service.

The Level I contract was changed for many of the employees. Level II team function was now competitive with win-lose behaviors, and it was no longer the functional centered team of the past. Interdepartmental groups were no longer functional aspects but market segments, and the resource cooperation of the past stopped abruptly. The reorganization at the interdepartmental group level had a significant side effect.

A major change occurred in the top management team. The vice-president for finance was an executive vice-president and was held to be senior in the interdepartmental group. His place and prestige shifted as the team shifted to a market-driven and market-competitive function. He was no longer the key player, and for various reasons the team did not spend time reviewing his area. The vice-president was responsible for investing both short term and long term to provide a significant amount of income to the health organization. Parts of the investments were in a savings and loan association with a high rate of return. This investment was not challenged and when the market turned sour due to the failure of the savings and loan, most of the principal of several million dollars as well as interest was lost, the organization came close to going under. The adaptability of Level IV had driven a change on Level III that could have proven fatal to the organization.

Summary

In this chapter we have anchored the multiple issues of organizational effectiveness and management on the four organizational levels. We have done this by separating task issues from relational issues, and by distinguishing content, process, and structure within the task and relational issues on each level. This framework enables managers and consultants to separate complex issues for the purposes of identification and appropriate intervention.

4

Interlevel Dynamics

The notion of organizational levels is common in organization development texts. The chapters of many OD texts are constructed around interventions at the different levels, for example, individual interventions, group interventions, intergroup interventions, and total system interventions (French and Bell, 1990). It appears that this approach uses organizational levels as a set of convenient headings under which to list various OD activities. Organizational levels in this context are a rather static notion. By contrast, we are endeavoring to describe the dynamic nature of the four organizational levels. A significant element in this dynamic nature is the relationship between levels. This relationship is grounded in the definition of each level in terms of the twin task—a task from within the level and a task from upper management's perspective. Therefore, when we talk about any particular level, we are simultaneously dealing with an interlevel reality. The systemic link between levels is also emerging in the related field of psychotherapy, whereby in the helping relationship between a client and a therapist, account is taken of the different levels of systems in which the client lives and participates and their effects on the client's life and perceptions (Barrett-Lennard, 1991).

The conceptual basis for the interconnectedness of organizational levels is found in systems dynamics (Senge, 1990). As Senge points out, the key insight in a systems approach is that interrelationships occur in feedback loops rather than linear cause-and-effect chains. Relationships are complex and not unidirectional. A manager's relationship with a work force is both affected and caused by the workers' reaction to the relationship. Within organizational systems, the interconnectedness of departments, functions, positions on the echelon, demonstrate the centrality of complex feedback loops. In the framework of the four organizational levels, each level is related to the other three. The individual is affected by his or her relationship to the team, the way the team works in the interdepartmental group, and the way the organization functions. The face-to-face team is affected by the way the individual functions in relation to the organization and vice versa, the way the interdepartmental group functions, and the success of the organization in its mission. The interdepartmental group is affected by how the organization relates to its environment, how its constituent teams function, and how the individuals and organization match their respective needs.

The interconnectedness between positions on the echelon and levels of complexity exists in the role of the key individual. The "key individual" is a general term to denote a person whose role crosses boundaries from one subsystem to another and links one subsystem to another (Likert, 1961). The team-leader, supervisor, manager, administrator crosses the boundary from individual area of responsibility to those of other functions or higher management. That is a crossing of boundaries on the hierarchical echelon. At the same time, these persons interact in interlevel dynamics. They bring individual issues to a team, and team issues to the interdepartmental group. When an individual represents a team to a broader function, he or she crosses from a team to an interdepartmental group level, and the dynamics of that interaction may lead to a reassessment of the individual level. Other interlevel interaction occurs in the "gatekeeping" role (Lewin, 1951; Allen, 1977; Ancona and Caldwell, 1988), whereby information is brought into the team from the external environment. New information brought by an individual, especially disconfirming information, may cause the team to reject the team messenger, thereby producing conflict in the team. We will return to the notion of the key individual in Chapter 6, when we examine how the process of change moves across the four levels.

Level I Effects on Other Levels

The bonding task at Level I implies an interconnectedness between the bonding partners. The individual brings life tasks to the organization and enters into a psychological contract with the organization. The feedback loop from the organization's management communicates that the person is of value and is worthy of compensation. The formal contract of employment is set up and enacted through conditions of employment, socialization, training and development, career planning, promotion opportunities, and other personnel management processes (Schein, 1978).

Dysfunctions at Level I can come from either side of the relationship. Issues particular to an individual can come from a person's maladaptive coping with the dynamics of the life, work, and family cycles of adult development (Schein, 1978). Managerial assumptions about human motivation, actual management behavior, and the conditions of employment and compensation create the conditions for, or inhibit, an effective Level I (McGregor, 1960; Schein, 1980; Weisbord, 1987; Argyris, 1990a).

Level I can affect any of the other three levels (Fig. 4.1). Depending on the individual's place in the organization's echelon this effect can be more or less significant. If a dysfunctioning on the individual level concerns the chief executive, then the Level

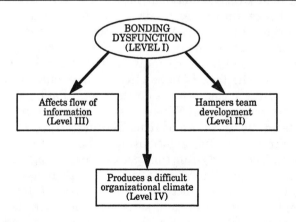

Figure 4.1
Level I Dysfunctions Affecting Other Levels

II top management team, the coordination of the entire organization at Level III, and the organization's competitive performance at Level IV are affected. When an individual level dysfunction occurs at the operational level, the effects may be more localized.

CASE: As we have already seen, Howard Head, as an engineer and CEO of Head Ski Company, turned management of the operation over to Harold Siegal and retained the engineering function for himself. But when production accelerated for greater output of skis, a higher rate of product failure occurred. Head reasserted his control as CEO and countermanded Siegal's decisions on changes used to increase production. The perspective of an engineer as understood in career anchor terms on Level I destroyed the management team (Level II). The Level III effect was conflict between production and sales. The effect of this conflict was also felt in the organization's competitiveness as other ski companies used the firm's crisis to boost their own competitive advantage (Level IV).

How Level I Affects Level II

As the individual enters into a face-to-face working team (Level II), issues of team membership predominate. The individual struggles to satisfy emotional needs—identity, power, control and influence, individual needs versus team goals, and acceptance-intimacy (Schein, 1988). The manner of resolving these issues on a continuing basis sets the psychological contract between the team and the individual member. From management's view, the task is to be effective in achieving the team's tasks, and the focus is more on uniting around common goals and effective processes. When team members do not integrate into a team the cause can be team dysfunction (Level II) or dysfunction in the bonding relationship at Level I among the team members. Yet if a dysfunction persists for a long time or does not yield to team process interventions, then most often the source is Level I dysfunction. We have already described how the ability of a manager to function as team leader deteriorated after the man developed an alcohol dependency, and how his team's work was adversely affected.

How Level I Affects Level III

As individuals interact with a wider and more complex system, depending on their position in the organization, there is a growing sense of alienation and of nonbelonging (Argyris, 1990a). The average individual's identification with his or her own team, section, or function typically means that the individual's interaction with the interdepartmental group primarily operates through membership in a team. As already mentioned, this scenario is different for key individuals, such as supervisors and middle and higher level management. In this context, Level III dynamics center around issues of information availability, resource allocation, and interteam power alignment as management attempts to orchestrate the aggregation of multiple teams at Level III. The career anchor can play a significant role when a technical interdepartmental group must interact with nontechnical departments to construct an information system.

For example, in the Head Ski case, the founder's technical-functional anchor colored his view of how the organization should function as he perceived it through an engineering perspective. In his Level II dealings with Siegal, the man he hired as general manager, he wanted to have a managerial counterpart that would dovetail with the engineering function. On Level III each function had its own operational role clearly defined and interlinked with other functions in a serial manner: Production, when it had completed its function, passed the issue on to Sales, which performed its role, and thus the product was passed on to the customer. That the functions did not participate in any interactive process was due to Howard Head's conceptual engineering approach. In the engineering approach product and process of manufacture were designed correctly to produce correctly so failure was impossible.

How Level I Affects Level IV

The chief executive of an organization plays a key role in forming the organization's strategic position in its external environment. We have opened a window on Howard Head in the company he founded and we will follow up with a view of Head in his role in the Prince Company in the next chapter. In each instance the leader's personality and career anchor are significant clues to the effect each will have on the organization. From the consultant's perspective, the career anchor is critical. An individual's anchor can color his or her view of how the organization should function. We have described how Head's technical-functional anchor was the force driving his view and management of the Head Ski Company.

CASE: In Transition University, as we discussed earlier, the past president operated in an authoritarian, top-down, detailed analysis mode. He worked that way himself, and his philosophy spread through the university. His successor worked from a participative model, whereby problem-solving and decision-making through consensus were implemented. His successor had an uphill battle in transforming the norm from the individual controlling his or her own area in isolation to one where interdependence created a need for interactive information-sharing and decision-making by consensus. This was apparent through all levels of the university as well as up and down the echelon. The twenty years' practice of guarding one's turf and working in isolation was difficult to overcome. The key individual's method of working had taken root in the organization culture.

This organizationwide behavioral pattern affected the organization's relationship with the external environment in significant ways. In athletics, a new facility had been erected. A major facility room, named the President's Locker Room, was limited to outside guests and to faculty who would pay a premium for its use. The faculty rebelled, distorting use of the facility. In Admissions, full scholarships were named Presidential Scholarships. They were ten per year, afforded full tuition, and were much more generous than other scholarships. The president personally wrote a note to each of the recipients accepting them to the university. Almost one third of the total funds used for tuition were dedicated to these ten scholarships, leaving the other 600 members of the class without sufficient tuition assistance from the university. This specialized, hands-on functioning of the institution rendered it less capable of competing with other institutions in the outside environment. The university was unable to respond to the external competition with other universities for students of good academic background. The internal reaction of guarding one's turf and trying to please the president became more determinative than the marketplace.

Level II Effects on Other Levels

Team dynamics occur throughout the organization from top management to the cleaning shifts. They are found in the workings of teams within each department, formal and informal committees, task forces, and so forth. The face-to-face team level is connected to the individual, interdepartmental group, and organizational levels (Fig. 4.2).

How Level II Affects Level I

A team's norms may result in behavior that discriminates against particular individuals and may create a team dysfunction with respect to the individual. A sales team of Long Distance Communications company included one woman in an otherwise all male team. Avid sports enthusiasts, the men constantly spoke in sports analogies and imagery. Barraged by sporting models, their female colleague, who had no interest in sports, felt that she was being made to feel inadequate. The lack of sensitivity on the part of the men forced the woman to withdraw psychologically from active participation in the team. When she explained the difficulties that she was having to her

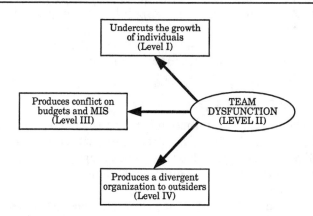

Figure 4.2
Level II Dysfunctions Affecting Other Levels

MBA organizational behavior professor, he suggested that she confront the team about their behavior and talk out the issues involved. The prospect of being able to raise and articulate the issues encouraged the woman to return to her team, confront the men with their behavior in a gentle way, and show how it produced a feeling of exclusion in her. While this confrontation resulted in some sensitivity and opened the door for greater participation in the team on the woman's part, it did not eclipse all the prejudice and behavioral practices that had built up in an all-male organization over a long period of time. In this therapeutic intervention, it was not a prescriptive solution that was brought to bear, but an awareness on the part of all concerned that a level playing field was required for participation in the team.

How Level II Affects Level III   In a large organization, the interdepartmental group's effectiveness depends on the quality and timeliness of information and resources from the teams that make up the interdepartmental group, so any interdepartmental group level dysfunction may be due to a particular team's dysfunction in achieving its tasks. For instance, when a finance department delays purchase or payment for purchases, new purchases are not received on time for particular projects. A finance team's context is always at the interdepartmental group and organizational levels: receiving information; providing it for other parts of the organization; making judgments regarding financial criteria for the operation (Level III), and relating it to external auditors, the board of management, and the CEO (Level IV).

How Level II Affects Level IV

The interlevel interaction between the team and organizational levels can be found in those teams whose role is to work on policy and strategy, such as top management teams, sales teams, and other boundary functional teams.

CASE: Modular Building Company's engineering division was going through a difficult period. Competitors were focusing on custom building, yet the company manufactured modular buildings. The engineering team met to determine how to deal with its problems. They called a meeting with the sales and manufacturing departments. In a separate venture that included the same people, Nicholas Rashford had acted as facilitator at a management training session. He again facilitated, engaging the participants in an exercise with tinker toys to encourage the development of team skills. The top management team elected to stay together as a group. As the exercise proceeded, the company's president got up, left the team, and began to pace the room on his own. He then returned to the team with an answer on what the team should use the toys to build and how it could sell the idea—the task of the exercise. The team complied. In the review and discussion that followed, it was reflected that the president's behavior in the exercise was his common way of behaving and that the company's top management team operated in this manner also. In fact, the real issue in the company's inability to develop custom building was that the divisions represented by top management wanted to do their work as individuals and did not have the skills to work together. Working together was essential in order to produce custom building for the customer.

Level III Effects on Other Levels

The interdepartmental group level is the most political of levels and it is here that interlevel interaction is most critical (Fig. 4.3).

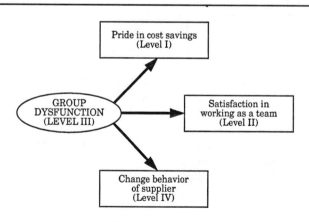

Figure 4.3
Level III Dysfunctions Affecting Other Levels

Interdepartmental group level dynamics are commonly enacted in team level settings where representatives of different functions or departments meet to coordinate and review plans and activities. Success at this level requires political maneuvering and bargaining in order to achieve adequate political balance between information availability, resource allocation, and the maintenance of power and influence of particular interests. An instance of the interdepartmental group level interacting with the individual level occurs when department heads experience blocking of their suggestions and proposals; their frustration at their inability to get ideas through leads them to withdraw from the arena and perhaps leave the organization.

How Level III Affects Level I

The effect of Level III on Level I is most often seen in the budgeting process or the management of information. The organization that finds resources scarce and begins to change the allocation process will soon affect one team more than another. Individuals begin to worry about their relationship with the organization. The ability of the organization to be a place of personal growth appears to diminish.

How Level III Affects Level II

CASE: The regional superior and the council of a religious order set up a committee to design and coordinate their members' education and training in social analysis and the spirituality of social justice as a central expression of Christian faith. After eighteen months' work the committee hired David Coghlan to meet them and help them assess themselves. It was reported that morale in the committee was low; one member had resigned and the others were on the point of following her. The consultant met the remaining members and inquired into the committee's work—its goals, its accomplishments, its way of working, and so on. What became apparent to the consultant from the report and discussion was that the committee had been very active and had fulfilled its brief fairly effectively. At the same time, its work did not seem to be having an impact on the religious order's membership as a whole. Many of their organized activities were not receiving adequate response. What emerged was that the committee had been somewhat marginalized within the system that had set it up. The regional superior and her council had established the committee, given it a mission they judged to be of high priority, and then handed over responsibility for its implementation. The consequence of this action was that the committee's work was perceived to be outside the mainstream of the order's activity, not connected to the hierarchy's actual priorities, and therefore, something on offer that could be taken or left as one judged. The consultant reflected this perception to the committee and it was decided that the committee would take the issues to the regional superior and her council for consideration. Some weeks later the consultant attended a meeting of the council and facilitated a review of the strategic role of the committee's work and the role to be played by the superior in being seen to own and direct the process.

This case illustrates the effect the lack of clarity on the part of the regional superior and her council had on the working of the social analysis committee. The dysfunction occurred on the regional Level III, where the establishment of the committee was not integrated into the integrated system of that religious order's regional government. Instead, the committee was left on its own, became marginalized within the system, and consequently its own Level II process began to deteriorate. The solution lay not in Level II team building within the committee, but in the Level III dynamics of the relationship between the committee and the wider system from which it received its mission and resources.

How Level III Affects Level IV

Interdepartmental rivalry or conflict can sabotage an organization's ability to compete in its external market. A labor dispute can cripple a firm when it loses its share of the market during a strike, or its good name for reliability may suffer so that when the dispute is ended the firm finds it difficult to recover its former position. The terms of settlement may put severe strain on the firm's resources.

CASE: Sometimes the effect of Level III on other levels is positive. For example, at Universal Greeting Card Company the manufacturing department, which used large quantities of paper purchased on rolls measured by the ton, set up an interdepartmental group management information system to detect paper losses throughout the production process. Each roll was purchased within parameters of length, thickness, and weight. The company wanted to increase its productivity by controlling and reducing the amount of waste. As the paper moved along the card production process, whenever presses were out of register or there were other failures, the length of paper that had to be scrapped was measured and detailed against the weight of the original roll. This led to reduction of waste. The printing foremen and their teams were put under pressure to curtail waste (Level III affecting Level II). At the same time, there was considerable tension between the production people and card design people as Production blamed Card Design for making designs that were difficult to print (Level III affecting Level II in another function).

The control of scrap and measurement of the length of paper to provide a better manufacturing control mechanism turned out to have the desired effect, but not in the way expected. The paper manufacturer, through its sales people who represented the firm to Greeting Card Company, heard that the card company was measuring the length of each roll in order to ascertain wastage. Fearful of losing the card company's business, the paper manufacturer evaluated its process and found it had allowed the paper to be produced thicker than it should be for one specified weight of roll. The resulting roll was shorter, producing fewer cards for the card company. The card company wanted length for more cards. The paper company changed its manufacturing process in order to produce a thinner paper with the same strength but longer length on the roll. As a consequence, the card company improved its productivity by thousands upon thousands of impressions, and hence produced more cards. This effect from the change at Level III affected Level IV in the card company by putting it in a better strategic position vis-à-vis its competitors. A change also happened in the paper manufacturing company. This is an example of an interdepartmental level of one organization effecting Level III change in another organization. The case is interesting because it demonstrates feedback from one organization to another and shows how the control or attempted control of a production process, when shared with a supplier, ended up with the supplier having a greater change impact on the organization than the internal change efforts that had caused so much interdepartmental group conflict in the original situation.

Level IV Effects on Other Levels

The organizational level depends on the individual, team, and interdepartmental group levels working adequately. The organization's attempt to exist, to survive, and to fulfill its mission in a competitive environment requires a strategic balance between the subsystems within it. It is contingent on coordination at the interdepartmental group level (Level III), so that the many departments, functions, and interest groups maintain a working relationship that contributes to the organization's ability to fulfill its mission (Level IV). Such a coordination depends on each team being effective in its own area of responsibility (Level II), which, in turn, depends on an adequate formal and psychological contract between the individual and the organization (Level I). (See Fig. 4.4.)

Often, Level IV dysfunction emanates from the competitive environment and then affects the other levels. When a radical shift in the market necessitates a change in the material, engineering and manufacturing functions are drastically affected.

How Level IV Affects Level I

A special relationship exists between the organizational policy level and the individual level. The individual's identification

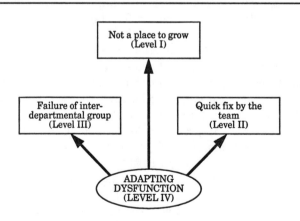

Figure 4.4
Level IV Dysfunctions Affecting Other Levels

with the organization's mission and culture depends upon how the organization functions in its external environment and how that filters back through the three levels. The ability to function at Level IV requires a sense of mission as well as stability and viability. When these are threatened, individuals review their most basic commitment to the organization. The relationship between these two levels is typically referred to as "organizational climate."

CASE: In a national health service, when funds from the exchequer were reduced in an effort to control public spending, there was less money to go around to the different sectors of the health service (Level III). This resulted in particular units receiving less money and having to work on reduced resources, both financial and personnel (Level II). Consequently, many units were placed under a great deal of strain. This in turn resulted in a growing anger and alienation among nursing staff, a decrease in the bonding relationship, and many seeking to leave the system and work elsewhere (Level I).

How Level IV Affects Level II

CASE: Environmental forces can play a significant part in the functioning of a top management team. An incoming regional council of a religious order spent a few days with a consultant at the outset of its term of office in which the critical environmental issues, both external and internal, were outlined. The team articulated its desired future for the region of the order, focused on critical issues in the present that needed to be changed, and mapped out the main paths for getting from the present to the desired future. The council's goals were set in terms of the change issues and the processes to be adopted to help it remain focused on those goals. Several years into the program, the team members have reported how valuable and useful it was to begin their term of office by focusing on the broader environmental picture, articulating a desired future, and establishing the work program in those terms. It was thought that such a focus gave the council members a good deal of energy for the work and enabled the council to work strategically, rather than get bogged down in day-to-day operational, problematic maintenance.

How Level IV Affects Level III

CASE: Head Ski Company, which became the industry leader by introducing aluminum skis, found itself being eclipsed by the French competitor that introduced fiberglass skis. Head's engineering department was threatened by this because it did not know how to work with the new material. The production department was threatened because it only knew how to work with aluminum, and Head himself was threatened because his specialty was aluminum skis. Yet the company continued to make aluminum skis. When Head took over the Prince Company, he made tennis racquets of aluminum. When graphite and other materials threatened, he hired new engineers who could work with graphite, integrated them into his team, and trained the sales force to adapt and sell graphite racquets. (The Prince case is developed in the next chapter.)

Summary

In this chapter we have shown how the four organizational levels are implicitly interconnected. Each level is linked to each of the others (Fig. 4.5). An understanding of how the loops feed back from one level to another is essential for the manager or consultant in assessing the workings of each level and in preparing interventions.

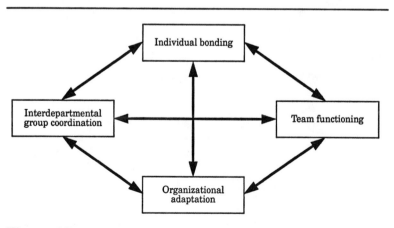

Figure 4.5
Interlevel Dynamics

5

The Process of Change

The organization development literature has typically analyzed the process of change without fully acknowledging the complexity that arises from the fact that change has to occur at each of the levels we have described so far (Lippitt, Watson, and Westley, 1958; Alderfer, 1976; Pugh, 1986; Blake and McCanse, 1991). What is often lost in the literature on change management is that while an organization undergoes change and is in the process of adaptation, it is made up of interdepartmental group subsystems that require coordination. These in turn comprise team level units that have functional tasks, which in turn are made up of individuals, bonded to the organization with individual needs in regard to the change. One cannot ignore the interlevel dynamics that occur as change at each level occurs.

In this chapter we will first present several generic models of change drawn from the OD literature; subsequent chapters show how the models apply to the total change process at the four organizational levels. We begin with the most basic general change, first articulated by Kurt Lewin (1951) and elaborated by Schein (1961, 1980, 1987).

The Lewin–Schein Change Process Model

Any change process can be conceptualized as consisting of three stages: a stage of unfreezing, a stage of moving, and a stage of refreezing. No change will occur unless the system is unfrozen, and no change will last unless the system is refrozen sufficiently.

Ottaway (1983) developed a taxonomy of change agents that articulated the different roles that enable change to occur in Lewin's three stages. He calls those who generate the need for change "change generators" and distinguishes "key change agents," "demonstrators," "patrons" and "defenders." The key change agents and demonstrators actively promote change by showing the need for it, while the patrons and defenders provide support. Those who help change take place he calls "implementors," distinguishing "external change implementors," "external-internal change implementors," and "internal change implementors." These roles distinguish those who are brought into the system as external consultants and those who work from within the system. Finally those who help stabilize the change he calls "change adopters," and distinguishing "early adopters," "maintainers," and "users." These reflect the roles whereby change is maintained within the system. Ottaway argues, through his taxonomy, that each role is necessary for the change process to progress from unfreezing through to refreezing.

Schein elaborated Lewin's model of change by describing the psychological processes that must occur at each stage.

Unfreezing Unfreezing, creating the motivation to change, is the most difficult stage of change. For effective unfreezing to occur the following elements must be present:

1. The present state is somewhat disconfirmed.
2. Sufficient anxiety or guilt is aroused because some goals will not be met or standards not be achieved.
3. Sufficient "psychological safety" is provided to make it unnecessary for the target individuals or teams to psychologically defend themselves because the disconfirming information is too threatening or the anxiety or guilt are too high.

The essence of an effective unfreezing process is a balancing of enough disconfirmation to arouse a sufficient level of anxiety or guilt, and to provide enough support, direction, and help so that the system feels sufficiently safe to confront and act on the problem. How the unfreezing occurs will vary with the circumstances.

Changing   What unfreezing does is motivate the change agent to look for new solutions that will bring things back into equilibrium and that will once again produce confirming information that things are "OK." Where previously information, ideas, suggestions, or even orders were ignored, once persons or a group are unfrozen, they are more likely to pay attention. They become active problem solvers because they are uncomfortable.

The energy then switches to finding ways of resolving the problems. Schein describes two fundamentally different ways that this can be done:

1. Scanning the environment until a new formulation is found and trying out various kinds of new behavior until something that works is found, or

2. Finding a role model or learning a new point of view through psychological "identification," learning by seeing the world through the eyes of a role model.

Refreezing   Once the system has solved the problem and puts a solution in place, there remains the problem of refreezing. Refreezing is more about ensuring the change survives than about creating stability. Two elements are prerequisites for the survival of change:

1. Systemic refreezing, where the change fits both the system as a whole and the different subsystems.

2. Relational refreezing, where the change is supported across the four levels—individual change is supported in the team, team change in the individual and the group, and organizational change in all three other levels.

Four Psychological Reactions to Change

We have two reflections from our experience on the Lewin–Schein change model. First, the unfreezing process is painful and generates a number of specific psychological responses that need to be analyzed. So further articulation of the elements within disconfirmation and the creation of psychological safety are useful. Second, in organizations the movement from unfreezing through changing to refreezing actually involves a complex journey through the four organizational levels. In this chapter we will develop these two points by describing four psychological stages of change—denial, dodging, doing, and sustaining (Fig. 5.1). In the following chapter we will show how these stages interconnect with the four levels in a seven-phase change process.

Stage 1: Denying the Need for Change

The denial stage begins when the data supporting a change are first brought into the organization and disconfirmation first starts. It can be a denial of the need for change in the face of others' assertion of the need to change or the denial of a need for change caused by environmental forces. This stage centers around processing information, disputing its value, relevance, or timeliness. The change agent may be anywhere in the organization and will meet with denial from above and below. If the

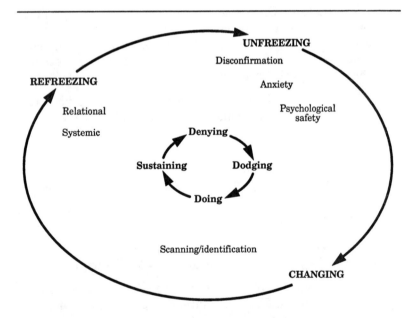

Figure 5.1
Stages of Change

change agent is a "change generator," either as "key change agent" or as "demonstrator" he or she will need the support of "patrons" and "defenders" to enforce the drive for change.

Resistance to change comprises cognitive and emotional elements that arise from the context of the change or the individual's inability to deal with change (Bunker and DeLisle, 1991). As Nevis (1987) argues, the starting place for dealing with resistance is to consider it as a healthy, self-regulating manifestation that must be respected and taken seriously by managers and consultants. Denial must be treated in this manner. On the cognitive dimension, the substantive issues of why change is needed, the degree of choice that exists about whether to change or not, the nature and strength of the forces driving change, the effect of the change on individuals and teams must be presented in such a manner that the individual can assess the perceived impact of the change in the light of full information. On the emotional dimension, managers and consultants need to listen to fears, empathize with different perspectives on the change, and create a climate that facilitates individuals' acknowledging and coming to terms with personal emotional forces that inhibit their participation in change. In short, for movement to occur there has to be sufficient psychological safety to allow the change data to be accepted as valid, relevant, and pertinent. In other words, some unfreezing must have begun.

At the same time, the acknowledgment of the need for change is somewhat generic. The acknowledgment that change is required is not necessarily internalized immediately. A reluctant acknowledgment shifts the impetus for change to other parts of the system. This is called a dodging. Some may remain in the denial mode and persist in denying that change is needed. But the change process may move on without them, and at a later stage those still denying the need for change will have to reassess their position.

CASE: In a case described in more detail in Chapter 6, we see a regional division of a Roman Catholic religious order attempt to initiate planned organizational change as a result of the Second Vatican Council by conducting a survey of needs of the country in which it ministers. The results of the survey were presented to several meetings of the senior members, in conjunction with research on the current and projected future state of existing ministries and personnel, and the necessity of transformational change was outlined. The need for transformational change was denied and countered with the scenario that things would fundamentally continue as they had been.

The regional superior set about establishing a renewal program to enable the system to unfreeze by focusing on individual development to meet the emotional issues and by setting up numerous task forces and commissions around specific policy areas to deal with the substantive issues (Friedlander and Schott, 1981). Over the following several years the agenda for change became established throughout the region and its members. However, many members continued to resist and refused to participate. While they might acknowledge the need for change in a general, theoretical way, they chose to remain outside the mainstream of developments. They in effect opted out, continued in their own mindset, and resented any attempts by superiors to change them. They continued their opposition, either by not attending meetings or by remaining silent at them and by complaining and voicing opposition at informal gatherings and among their peers. In subsequent years, as the change momentum became more established and as change took place, this group decreased in number, as some gradually began to participate in the changed organization and others retired. Some chose to remain outside.

Stage 2: Dodging

The preceding case illustrates the essential difference between the denial and dodging stages within unfreezing. The dodging stage begins when the accumulated evidence shows that the change is likely to take place. It is acknowledged reluctantly that some change is needed, but that the change is required in other parts of the system: "Others have to change" is a typical reaction. There can be a searching for countervailing data, which allows the individual or team to avoid or postpone having to change. On the emotional dimension, anger is expressed, typically in passive-aggressive nonparticipation. The anger is directed toward the change agents, with a more specific direction than the anger that might occur at the denial stage. At the dodging stage the anger is directed at "those who are making *me* change." Effort is devoted to diverting the change or at least finding some way to be peripheral to it.

On the cognitive dimension, an individual or team can confuse the issue by presenting the weakness of the approach to the change. There may be a more serious issue that needs to be dealt with first. This attempts to shift the action to a different focus. Another method to subvert change is to change its form. If the discussion is on work flow change, the dodger changes the topic to personnel. If the discussion concerns personnel, the dodger changes it to bulk capital budget funding or to the expense budget.

The generic approaches to dealing with resistance outlined under denial are also applicable to the dodging stage. The issues on the cognitive and emotional dimensions must be dealt with through a process of consultation, listening, and serious consideration of the concerns expressed. Movement beyond the dodging stage comes either when, as a result of consultation, ownership of the need for change is accepted and the change process can begin, or after some time has elapsed, when others have been implementing the change and the implications and effects of the change are perceived differently and perhaps appreciated or at least perceived less negatively. In terms of the Lewin–Schein model, the elements of disconfirmation, the presence of sufficient guilt or anxiety, and the creation of psychological safety are present so unfreezing has occurred.

Stage 3: Doing

The doing stage occurs when people have acknowledged and owned the need for change to the degree that they begin to explore what changes are required, how, where, at what cost, and at what cost to whom. The doing stage is not composed of any one action; it is a whole series of actions—diagnosing the forces driving and restraining change, interpreting data, articulating a desired future, having intermediate stages, creating and following a change plan, generating commitment, managing the transition, negotiating and bargaining, implementing, reviewing, and so on (Beckhard and Harris, 1987; Beckhard and Pritchard, 1992; Coghlan, 1990a). It may be spread over a considerable time. In terms of Ottaway's taxonomy (1983), the focus moves from the "change generators" to the "change implementors." As the change process unfolds, the issues are where change must occur in the present system, how that change should be made, and what cost must be diagnosed, decided upon, and implemented. The change process, whether utilizing a scanning, role identification, or a combination of both, tests the readiness and capability of the system to change.

Within a complex system, the change process necessitates dealing with controversy and disagreement regarding different diagnoses, negotiation and bargaining within the system, and dealing with the conflict that inevitably arises in such a context. Conflict at the doing stage is more focused than at the denial and dodging stages because it occurs within the context of a change plan. The issue is not whether change is required, but what change is required in which parts of the system and affecting which subsystems. Indeed on particular issues regarding possible solutions to a change problem, there may be a reversal to denial and dodging. Each proposal may initiate its own change stages. Therefore within the broader change process, several particular proposals may generate denial and dodging and need to be dealt with in those terms.

There are three courses the doing stage can take. One is an optimistic course, a matter of jumping on the bandwagon of change. More common is the second course, whereby doing involves negotiating what changes take place, how, and at what cost. The third course leads to a sense of futility that despite a lot of activity, the change does not address the real issues. At the moment when action should give a sense of satisfaction, there is an undercurrent that the organization has no identity or is losing its identity or value. It is at this point that the change issue may alter to encompass a more fundamental transformation of the organization. We will take up this point in the following chapter.

In the religious order, a momentum of reviewing policy through commissions and task forces, creation of policy development options, reviewing ministries, retraining, reallocation of personnel, and team building, involving most of the members of the region, became normative after the initial years of unfreezing. It was acknowledged more widely that change was not only needed but desirable, and the members largely participated, with differing levels of enthusiasm and commitment, in the region's change process.

Stage 4: Sustaining

As normative behavior is difficult to change, some reinforcement of changed habits is necessary to ensure change survives and the change state is sustained. This is the *refreezing* stage, when the "change adopters" come into prominence (Ottaway, 1983). The successful completion of this stage is the integration of the change into the habitual patterns of behavior and structure.

For the individual the new state must be reinforced by how the change fits the personality and is supported by significant others. This reinforcement constitutes the psychological basis of rewarding the continuance of the change state. For the individual members of the religious order, the changes were sustained through internalizing a new understanding of what it meant to be a minister in the church in the latter part of the twentieth century in the light of a developing theology and spirituality of ministry. These ministries were finding some expression in the organizational changes that were taking place.

In organizational terms, this stage is best defined as the *implementation* of operating procedures and is a key stage of any change process. It is the focusing of energy to follow through on programs and projects. Sometimes new manners of proceeding, new information systems, or even new endeavors mark this stage. At this point the organization needs to be attuned to the fact that change is part of life. The organization will have in place the ability to sense changes in the environment and to adapt quickly to them (Schein, 1980). In this respect, sustaining or refreezing does not attempt to create a new stability or close down future change, but it maintains an openness to continuous forces for change.

We have presented two core models of change that are relevant to the understanding and management of organizational change. A third model of change that is equally important distinguishes different degrees of change for any system, whether individual, team, or organizational. As a knowledge of these degrees of change is essential and is evident from the cases under consideration in this and the following chapter, we will now outline briefly some of the concepts in this regard.

Second-Order Change

The literature on planned change identifies two forms of change: first- and second-order change (Levy, 1986; Bartunek and Moch, 1987; Bartunek and Louis, 1988). According to Levy, "first-order change" refers to changes in one or two dimensions of an organization's activity, changes on one or a few levels (individual and team levels), a change in one or two behavioral aspects, improvements and developments in the direction already set, incremental changes, logical and rational change, reversible change, changes that do not alter the world view, and change within the old state of being. Argyris (1990b) uses the term "single-loop learning" to describe the ordinary learning acquired in finding solutions to problems. It aims at correcting things that aren't functioning by detecting the source of the problem, inventing a solution, implementing the solution, and evaluating its effect. Such learning is based on a linear line of inquiry: "If this, then." It is an essential form of learning for routine tasks and problems.

"Second-order change" refers to multidimensional and multilevel change. It changes all the behavioral aspects—attitudes, values, norms, perceptions, beliefs, world view, and behavior. It is primarily a qualitative change that is irreversible. It results in a new world view and a new state of thinking and acting (Levy, 1986). For Argyris (1990b), double-loop learning is the process of learning how to learn, of inquiring into what is being learned, and of questioning fundamental assumptions.

Second-order change, therefore, is synonymous with cultural change in that it is constituted by change in basic assumptions. This level of change is very complex and difficult because what is being changed is invisible and preconscious (Schein, 1992). Because culture is deeply embedded in groups, it is insufficient to attempt change only through the individuals of an organization's echelon. Second-order change needs to become embedded in the collective identity of teams, the group, and the organization, in other words, Levels II, III, and IV.

The realization by key individuals in an organization that an adaptation is inadequate may be a sign forewarning the need for a more transformational change, indeed for a wholly different organization.

The Near Failure of the Prince Company

CASE: After Howard Head sold Head Ski Company, he began to play tennis. He tells the story in his own words,

> After I retired in 1969, one of the things I did was build a house. While you're building a house you might as well put in a swimming pool. While you're putting in a swimming pool you might as well put in a tennis court. Once you have a tennis court you might as well learn to play tennis, which I had never played before. I found that it was not as easy as I thought. When I would swing the racquet, not having very good eye-hand coordination, I would hit off-center and the racquet would do this or that, which is very unpleasant on your arm, and also you don't get any balls back across the net. I took a ton of tennis lessons and it didn't do me any good. My instructor finally said, "Head, why don't you get a ball machine to practice against?" Now this was a decisive piece of luck in my life. Again, I'm going to emphasize that what happened to me *happened*—it wasn't planned. If he hadn't happened to say, "You need a tennis ball machine," then the Prince racquet never would have happened.
>
> There were two basic things about the machine. One, I thought it was a brilliant and ingenious piece of engineering—I just loved it. It was a machine that dropped balls into a hole from a rotor; compressed air would push the ball up into a barrel and shoot it out at you. I thought it was perfectly beautiful. I could empathize completely with the kind of guys who would have developed this, because I was one of them. It was right up my alley; it was an entrepreneurial-type machine. The other thing was that it was so full of bugs as to be totally worthless. So right away I thought, "I envy you guys; you're so good, but I'll tell you what: it's no damn good. The clapper valve doesn't work; this jams and it sticks; the motor conks out." To make a long story short, I went up to see [the machine's manufacturer]. Within one month I was chairman of the board and 25 percent owner of the company.

Level II Background

Howard Head's relationship with the management team at the Prince Company was best exemplified by his first interaction with them. By his own statement, he asked them to ship him a tennis ball machine by truck while he mailed them a check. He continued to deal with the company at arm's length, even as the firm's new board chairman, working as an outside consulting engineer. He reviewed the whole tennis ball throwing machine and made considerable adjustments that ended by making it a much better seller. This endeared him to both the engineering force and the sales department at the Prince Company.

After finding out that the ball machine only improved his tennis skills to a certain point, Head began to fiddle with the racquet. By changing its balance and size, he brought about a revolution in the tennis world similar to the one he had achieved in the ski world. Head redesigned the tennis racquet to increase the area of its playing surface. The new racquet was taken to the rules committee of the United States Tennis Association, who determined it to be legal. Head then got the patents on the new racquet. When it came time for Head to introduce the new tennis racquet, he went to the board as an outsider and presented the design in order to get the board's concurrence on building and marketing the product. Both Head and the board realized that the technology for building tennis racquets was available and that the Prince Company need not purchase machinery or set up an inside manufacturing process in order to proceed. They realized that they could detail the specifications and subcontract all of the production to an outside manufacturing source, which they did. Phenomenal growth of the organization then occurred. The company doubled its sales every six months after introduction of the wide-faced tennis racquet. Even though the company was mushrooming, sales were strong, and the product was the most talked about thing in the tennis world, the fact that professional tennis players would not use the racquet irked Head.

Stage 1: Denial This disconfirming information distressed Head and he tried to introduce product price control as a method to change sales and profitability, on the rationale that if the Prince racquet were the most expensive then it would be perceived to be the best. In the ski industry the highest priced skis were Head skis. In the racquet market with only one material and size, retail outlets were using the Prince racquet to bait and switch. They would advertise the Prince racquet at a lower price, get people into the store, and then point out that another size or material would be better for that particular tennis player, thus selling a competitor's product. What Head was denying at this juncture was that he was attempting to replicate Head Ski Company in the Prince Company.

After numerous unsuccessful attempts to change the situation by sales or product maneuverings, Head decided to hire a new President and chief operating officer for Prince. He chose a major head hunting firm and sat down with them to prepare a job description for the position and set out the background characteristics of the individual to fill the position.

Stage 2: Dodging He asked me [Nicholas Rashford] to go along: "Nick, this will be good for your education. You will learn how the real nonacademic world works." Howard did not accept help in putting together a description for the position. His idea of what he was looking for in the president of the Prince Company gives us an idea of what was going on in his mind. Here are excerpts from the position description:

> **DUTIES:** The President and Chief Operating Officer will report to the Chairman of the Board and Chief Executive Officer, Howard Head, along with the Vice Chairman. This group of three officers will constitute the Office of the Chairman and they will together develop the long-range strategy for Prince, outline the operating policy to implement that strategy, and generally provide the creative force for continued growth. In addition to being part of the Office of the Chairman, the new President will have direct day-to-day operating responsibilities for sales, operations, manufacturing, and engineering. Player relations and international marketing will report to the Vice Chairman.
>
> **EXPERIENCE:** 10 years
>
> **EDUCATION:** College degree; M.B.A. a moderate plus
>
> **OTHER CHARACTERISTICS:** The individual sought should be bright, sharp, and detail-oriented in the mold of a successful financial professional. Imagination in terms

of product ideas is not as important as creativity in the way the organization is managed and problems solved. This person must enjoy detail as well as interacting with people of high imagination and intellect while being close to a perfectionist in implementation. Rather than be a desk-bound administrator, this individual must be one who becomes personally involved in all details of the business, particularly in connection with product and product development. A sense of design and an intuitive mechanical comprehension are required. An interest in, and ability to comprehend, the tennis marketing world would be desirable. Good legal sense, coupled with horse-trading savvy and follow-through will be valued assets. Should be able to gain acceptance in a group.

As a consultant at arm's length with Head in the executive search, I had no doubt that he was set on changing the presidency and CEO. We sat through a full day's interviews and no one made the grade. It became apparent to me that no one ever would. More than twenty prospects were reviewed. The day ended in great frustration.

During the evening hours at his hotel Head's frustration turned to raw anger. The more he expressed anger, the more the historical perspective of Head's past career at the ski company came to mind. Together we had relived that in doing a live case in two classes a semester for almost five years. The frustration he voiced toward Prince's president was the same as he had voiced in class toward his choice of president at Head Ski. I confronted Head with the unfinished business at Head Ski. Howard was angry at his successor, Hal Siegal, at whom he voiced rage and blame over the loss of the ski company. The process shifted and Head began to realize that the change process he wanted was a different Prince Company. At this juncture Head had unfrozen with regard to understanding the core change issues and was ready to act.

Stage 3: Doing   Head wanted a sales-driven tennis racquet company and not a production-oriented, ball-throwing-machine manufacturing company. When asked what sort of a company he wanted, he started to detail a mission statement and a set of common goals and objectives for the company. The head hunter was canceled and we returned to Baltimore and worked on the mission statement and set objectives for the new Prince Company. Here follows the output of that effort. The process took several days and long nights. It was evident that Head had a very clear idea of what he wanted.

Overall Objectives

Fulfill Prince's destiny as the racquet of the 1980s. To do so the Prince Company must keep itself super sharp in *all* departments. Its objectives will be excellence in everything it does. It will limit itself to what it knows best— namely, tennis racquets. For example, the ball machine is okay if it does not take too much energy of the organization from the manufacture of racquets. New tennis strings will be appropriate and important. Other accessories that can carry the Prince name like balls, sweatshirts, bags, etc., are okay if they are understood to be largely for promotional purposes and not for a profit motive. The idea of franchising our name for use on tennis clothes is okay provided the quality is high enough and that it does not involve any corporate energy. In other words, to repeat, our emphasis will remain on the Prince tennis racquet.

The company will strive to be totally excellent in all its endeavors and in all its operations and functions. Excellent both in *quality* of performance and in *scope* of performance.

After the company objectives were spelled out in what was in effect a mission statement, Head then worked on the statements for each department. They contain quite a bit of detail, as can be seen from the following excerpts:

Objective: Improve Telemarketing

Establish a warm, fatherly (or motherly) contact with all our dealers. A warm image, a feeling of personal caring. For example: A phone call to every dealer at least once a month asking him how he is doing, any problems, anything we can do to help. Any complaints. Develop in all our phone personnel a warm, friendly, supportive manner. Do this regardless of whether or not the shop is already being called on by our commission reps.

Develop and expand this objective to its maximum usefulness. The budget should be insignificant in comparison to the results.

Again, while this program will increase our sales, we should consider its primary purpose to spread a warm, strong, good, happy, excited, friendly feeling toward Prince: "Boy, those people at Prince really are nice people!"

Objective: Tune-up of Customer Service

Develop our customer service contacts to generate the same sort of feeling described in the Telemarketing Objective. Every caller receives a friendly, smiling, fatherly (or motherly), good-humored (and when appropriate, sympathetic), interested, and caring response. The response from the customer must come to be always, "Boy, those Prince people really are great to talk to. I was surprised!"

Be well prepared to get along with the customer even when he is manipulating us or pulling a fast one, or trying to get away with something—when it serves our purpose to do so! The secret here would be to train our people to give the guy what he wants but with a manner so that he knows he isn't fooling us but that we are nevertheless wanting to be friendly and generous.

Advertising Objectives

Howard Head developed specific objectives for the outside ad agency as well:

Develop a uniform advertising thrust to establish Prince as the racquet of the day, *the* racquet of the future. The "now" racquet. The "prestige" racquet. The racquet to be proud of. The new generation racquet. The Prince generation racquet. The racquet that's making <u>everyone</u> play better.

Stage 4: Sustaining   These objectives were taken back to the Prince Company. We presented them to the existing president and got his concurrence and we saw his relief. He embraced what Howard Head wanted and set about putting it in place. From this point on, the Prince Company was very successful.

Another change took place shortly thereafter. Prince had contracted out most of the racquet manufacturing, thus saving the tooling costs that others had already expended. With patents it was easy to prevent other firms from making the same racquets, yet as competitors, they were doing the manufacturing for Prince. When the young engineers at Prince proposed the idea of using graphite for construction of the racquet, Head embraced the concept and worked with them to design the new racquets. Again others were contracted to manufacture these racquets and a new era in tennis was born. Later Prince was sold to Cheseburo Ponds.

Reflections on the Case

Level I Effects While the study of the Head Ski Company case is fascinating in terms of organization development, the opportunity to compare it to a second company influenced by the same CEO adds to our knowledge base. There are few cases of two such successful companies led by the same key individual. Head found it hard to deal with the CEO and stepped in to resume his duties on three different occasions in the Head Ski Company. His actions were driven by what was going on within Level I. It was difficult for Head not to have control of all the different processes: from design to engineering to manufacturing—even to design of the marketing copy. It becomes obvious that what Head was trying to do was to mold each and every detail of the organization to his way of doing things. All of this was driven by his need to have the Head skis or the Prince tennis racquet be used by the sport's professionals and be found the best that could be made—because each was an extension of Howard Head himself.

Level II Effects Howard Head modified this dominant stance somewhat by trying to remain somewhat distant from the organization geographically if not in spirit. The Prince Company was located in Princeton, New Jersey, while Head maintained his residence in Baltimore, Maryland. He had to ride the train for 2½ hours to reach the company's headquarters. As he suggests, this was at Nicholas Rashford's urging as a consultant:

"Nick told me later it was lucky for me that it was not in Baltimore or I would probably have destroyed the company—with my kind of personality. It was lucky for me that it was located in Princeton, New Jersey, 200 miles away so that I only went up there a couple of days every couple of weeks."

We learn from the comparison of these two organizations that, on Level I, personality development and orientation—how Head looked at the world around him—had an impact on both of the companies he led. It affected the Level II relationship with the president or manager in each case. They had to define the common elements in the relationship.

Level III Effects   Head's view of himself and the world defined the functional relationships of the organization, always in engineering terms, so that the relationship between each of the functions—production, sales, marketing—always had to dovetail in a very exact way. Decisions on such basics as the use of material, aluminum versus fiberglass or graphite, because of Head's engineering background, become consistent throughout both situations. The use of "pros" to show the qualifications and the value of the end product—the use and endorsement of the racquet and the skis by experts—were both critical to Head's self-esteem and identity with his companies.

Level IV Effects   On one issue related to the organization adapting to the external environment, Head had learned a lesson from the experience of his ski company. There was a move to graphite in the competitive environment, the tennis rachet marketplace. This was a big challenge for Howard Head and for Prince. If he had resisted as he had the introduction of fiberglass at the Head Ski Company, he would have generated a very different outcome and not a success story. Head moved to this new material. He got involved in understanding its molecular structure as well as designing the extrusion and other manufacturing processes for fabricating racquets out of graphite.

The Benefits of a Levels Analysis

The preceding review points out the benefit of an analysis of organization development through the use of *levels theory*. The case is also a strong example of second-order change. Head's denial was normal in the context of the second-order change. His anger was appropriate to the frustrations he felt from an intuition that something was wrong at Prince. The president at Prince dodged because he could not see a transitional state, let alone see an outcome state. These forces, when they are so much more intense, are indicative of a need of second-order change. The purpose of the change is not to sell more product or make it better but to bring into existence a new generation of the company.

For the leader, physical distance was important to keep from destroying the company with his intensity and drive. Yet when it came time to envision a new company, that same intensity was a positive force for change. When the "do it" stage began, the quickness of response was astounding. Prince turned itself into a very skillful marketing company in a very short time. Young engineers saw the materials change in the works and got Head on board. They created a second new organization based on graphite racquets.

Summary

The framework of the four organizational levels adds an essential dimension to change theory. First, it distinguishes the tasks and issues at each level, which become more intense and focused in a change situation. For the manager and consultant, diagnosis of change issues demands acknowledging coordination on Level III, face-to-face functioning of teams on Level II, and bonding between individual and organization on Level I as discrete issues for understanding and intervention. Second, the interdependence of the four levels illustrates the necessity of conscious management of the effect that a change on one level has on the other levels. So a triggering event on Level II must be dealt with on Level I, Level III on Levels II and I, and Level IV on all three. Third, organizational resistance found during the levels analysis or the failure to get a fit between levels can often be an indicator, for the first time, of a need for second-order change.

6

Phases and Levels of Organizational Change

As the change process moves through an organization, a domino effect occurs: The key change agent takes the change issue to a team, the team takes it to the interdepartmental group, and so on until the change affects the entire organization, both internally and externally. The unfreezing, changing, and refreezing in a complex system involves individuals and teams hearing the news of the proposed change, reacting to it, and deciding how to respond. What is required is that there is a critical mass whose support is needed for movement to occur and change to take place (Beckhard and Harris, 1987).

We will now detail how the reactions to change interact with the four levels. Myriad activities and interactions must occur in a large systems change process, but we have grouped many of them together to form a seven-phase sequence to simplify explanation of the process (Table 6.1). The phases map the movement of the change process through an organization— across the four levels taking account of how individuals, teams, the interdepartmental group, and the organization deny and dodge change before doing.

CASE: In the previous chapter we introduced the case of a region of a religious order that embarked on a long-term change process in the light of change inspired in the Roman Catholic Church by the Second Vatican Council (1962–65). We will now continue with this case as it illustrates something of the pattern of how change moves across the four organizational levels through several identifiable phases. A further case illustration will be presented in Chapter 7.

Table 6.1
Phases and Levels of Organizational Change

Phase 1: Disconfirmation	
Key individual	Denying, dodging
Phase 2: Initiation	
Key Individual	Doing
Team members	Denying, dodging
Phase 3: Maneuvering	
Key individual	Doing
Team members	Doing
Interdepartmental group members	Denying, dodging
Phase 4: Integration	
Key individual	Doing
Team members	Doing
Interdepartmental group members	Doing
Organization	Denying, dodging
Phase 5: Action	
Key individual	Sustaining
Team members	Doing
Interdepartmental group members	Doing
Organization	Doing
Phase 6: Follow-through	
Key individual	Sustaining
Team members	Sustaining
Interdepartmental group members	Doing
Organization	Doing
Phase 7: Sustaining	
All	Sustaining

Phase 1: Disconfirming

The Key Individual Denying and Dodging

Change enters the organization through an individual, a "generator" (Ottaway, 1983). Commonly that person at first reacts to the need for change by denying the validity, relevance, and pertinence of the data calling for change. Once that person recognizes that the need for change does apply, he or she may dodge the issue and leave to others the matter of acting on the insight. This gives way to a realization that the information calling for change is real and threatening, that the organization is in peril if something isn't done. The key individual at this instance can be anywhere in the organization and, in effect, performs the role that Allen (1977) describes as a "technological gate keeping" and Ancona and Caldwell (1988) describe as "scouting"—bringing to the team from the environment the special information the team needs to perform its task.

The individual who perceives the need for change may not be a key individual in the organization's hierarchy. Duties at the strategic level involving analysis of market trends may have led him or her to question how the organization is currently functioning. That person may have direct contact with customers or clients and bring feedback to the organization on the organization's product or services. If not a key individual, then that person must approach a key individual (manager, team leader) and persuade him or her to take on the change issue. The message from the first person to perceive the need for change may have to pass through several layers of the organization's hierarchy before it reaches a key individual powerful enough to act on it. At each juncture the individual presented with the change issue goes through the initial reactions of denial and dodging before reaching the stage of doing and acting on the information. If the key individual is threatened by the change issue or by the messenger's approach, the change process may be blocked and proceed no further. Ownership by the key individual powerful enough to decide that the issue is one to be acted on concludes this phase.

CASE: In the case of the religious order, the regional superior, prior to his appointment, attended some meetings and courses that transformed his thinking about the need for change in the religious order and the role of leadership in the change process. He learned that change had to be led from the top so he became determined to use his leadership role in creating change. At this stage he had unfrozen and was prepared to lead change in a directive manner.

Phase 2: Initiation

The Key Individual Doing and the Team Denying and Dodging

When the key individual has worked through the psychological reactions of denial and dodging regarding the change issue, he or she moves to the "doing" stage. This means presenting the change data to the appropriate team for consideration and action, emphasizing the necessity for change, and beginning to define the dimensions of the change required. The person emphasizes why change is necessary at this time, as well as the degree of choice and the ultimate control over the change (Beckhard and Harris, 1987). The process of denying and dodging is repeated in the team as the individual members deny that change is required and dodge (We don't have to do it *now*) before entering a period of bargaining. The tendency to shoot the messenger who has brought the bad news must be recognized. This phase is concluded when the team, as a unit, recognizes the issue as critical and then acknowledges the need to do something. Ownership of an articulated problem ends this phase, not just as defined by an individual, but as articulated by the team through consensus. There will be individuals who do not support the change but are not powerful enough to block or stop it.

CASE: On assumption of his office, the regional superior was determined to generate change in the region. There were two commissions, set up by his predecessor, which were concluding their work. One had been conducting a survey of the needs in the environment and the other had been reviewing the order's existing ministries in the region and the present and future state of manpower resources. The regional superior decided to use the occasion of the completion of the two commissions' work as the entry point for change. He persuaded his advisors and team that the work of the two committees was the catalyst of initiating change.

Phase 3: Maneuvering

The Key Individual and Team Doing, and the Interdepartmental Group Denying and Dodging

The maneuvering phase involves bringing multiple teams together at the interdepartmental group level to confront the issue of the change. Denial first and then dodging are repeated within the individual teams that make up the interdepartmental group. Each team tends to see the change issue from its own viewpoint and may deny the validity, relevance, and pertinence of the change. It will be evident in the organization that at Level III some functions will have to diminish and some will have to grow, that some teams are more critical than others, that some activities will be let go and others developed.

The rationale behind the denial may focus on the information system, claiming that the present form of data gathering is not providing the information that would lead to change. Denial at the interdepartmental group level typically means the emergence of differing and conflicting interpretations of the data supporting the change. People may claim that the information driving the change is not accurate or reliable and is open to differing interpretations. The political relationship between teams may be a factor in denial, as, for instance, when one team denies the need for a change that is being promoted by a rival team. Subcultures within the organization may assert their history and tradition to block change (Schein, 1992).

Questioning of the decision support system is a common form of dodging. This occurs when coordination of the interdepartmental group is not effective and teams blame each other for inefficiencies. Dodging needs to be addressed by internal mapping processes. The interfacing of teams is the most relevant area of trouble. To promote ownership of change it is critical to get teams to see the problem in a new way. Mapping work flow is a means of extending the boundary of the group's search for information to solve a problem. Each functioning team must be conscious of what others do and how, and the way their own actions affect and are affected by what others do. Dodging at this stage is often expressed by the comment, "If everyone else did their work my team would have no problems." This phase ends with agreement on articulation of the problem and the steps needed to introduce change. Typically, reaching this agreement involves correctly identifying the critical people needed to make the change and describing the desired new steady state (Beckhard and Harris, 1987; Beckhard and Pritchard, 1992; Coghlan, 1990a).

In contract renewals with labor unions, articulating bargaining outcomes is a prelude to negotiation. Once collective bargaining between management and unions is undertaken, the interdepartmental group is at the "doing" stage. Collective bargaining negotiates what changes will takes place, how, at what cost, and to whose benefit. This phase concludes with ownership of the change and of the effect the change will have on the organization's stakeholders, both internal and external.

Denying and dodging are natural reactions to the unexpected news that change is needed. They are two phases in the unfreezing process as experience is disconfirmed and anxiety is felt (Schein, 1961, 1980, 1987) (Fig. 5.1). Because change involves movement away from what is familiar and accepted, it is threatening and stressful. It is not surprising that the initial reaction to change is that change is not necessary, and, as we have seen, that such a reaction typically shifts to avoidance or dodging. As Schein points out, the critical issue for movement from dodging to doing is the creation of psychological safety. The doing and changing stages are complementary, as are the refreezing and sustaining stages. Schein's notion of relational refreezing can be understood in terms of the four organizational levels in harmony, sustaining a change.

In our experience there is a danger of regression, particularly at Phases 2 and 3. As the key individual experiences the team's denial and as the team experiences the interdepartmental group's denial it is often noticed that the individual or the team can lose confidence and slip back into a dodging mode. The presence of a consultant can be significant in confronting this tendency and in helping the manager and the team process what is going on and remain firm in their convictions.

CASE: In the case of the religious order, the regional superior presented the findings of two commissions (one that had surveyed environmental needs and the other that had reviewed existing ministries and manpower) to a representative meeting of the region's senior members. His approach was to emphasize the changing nature of the environment (as expressed in the needs survey) and to support his argument with the data on the region's limited resources and declining manpower. He invited participation in decision-making about the future and the comprehensive change which, in his view, faced the order. In organizational levels terms, he attempted strategic change on Level IV to a Level III representative gathering. The response was largely one of denial. The participants at the meeting denied the need for fundamental change, defended their own constituencies from the threat of such change, asserted that what had been done before could continue, and effectively blocked change.

The superior felt isolated and wanted to resign. The superior-general of the order gave him unqualified support to continue. The regional superior analyzed the situation and decided to initiate a large personal development program through which many members participated in sensitivity training and similar experiential learning based programs in order to promote the individual and enable individuals to grow in self-awareness—a Level I directed intervention.

At the same time an OD consultant was hired to gather the members' feedback on how they saw the organization. After a frank report was published, the superior, with the consultant's help, established an internal consultancy team to help bring about change. A number of task forces were set up with members of the region serving on them, and the consultancy team provided a service by doing research and facilitating meetings. During the three years of this work, there was a gradual movement toward recognizing that change was inevitable (movement from denial), though many attempted to opt out and others left it to the superior to keep the pressure on (dodging).

As was the custom in the religious order, the regional superior completed his six-year term of office and a new person took office. He initiated team-building workshops and mandated ministry teams and communities to hold meetings on particular topics with external consultants present. Over a two-year period he attempted to facilitate the development of team skills (Level II) as a natural follow-on to the sensitivity training and to integrate the content of the change issues into the process. He emphasized co-responsibility and participation in the process of change. Over his six years the threat that change posed appeared to lessen. The change agenda was now established and was integrated into the ongoing process of the region.

Phase 4: Integration

The Key Individual, Team, and Interdepartmental Group Doing, The Organization Denying and Dodging

The organization's adaptive behavior commences at the point when organizational change forces its impact on the organization's external functioning and relations. An initial question in this phase is how other organizations and stakeholders will perceive themselves and the organization if the change is introduced. Assumptions about the interrelatedness of competitive organizations are questioned. At first such interrelatedness may be denied, but when it is accepted, the question is: "What is the least amount of change acceptable?" Accurate competitive analysis leads to accepting the notion of interlinking of organizations in competitive markets. The open systems planning approach maps the impact of the changed and changing organization on its customers or clients, competitors, and the market in general. The organization will be involved in extensive marketing activities in order that the changed organization's products or services will meet customers' or clients' needs. Successful change requires an understanding of the stakeholders' demands and behavior and a proactive stance in their regard.

CASE: In the religious order, the third regional superior in this sequence went about articulating a strategic plan. He openly declared his intention, set up groups across the region to draft policy statements on the main areas, articulated and emphasized the process to be followed, and actively led the process himself. It was an active doing stage on Level III as the region was confronted with policies and decisions touching each sector of the region. The outcome was an integrated strategic plan that articulated the order's mission, the environmental needs, the order's resources, the decisions, and the action steps (Level IV) (Coghlan, 1987). At this juncture the change was still in the internal organization at Level III. The order had not yet brought the change to its stakeholders, which had its traditional expectations of what and how the order conducted its ministries.

Phase 5: Action

The Key Individual Sustaining, the Team, Interdepartmental Group and Organization Doing

The key individual goes into a sustaining stage when energy is no longer required to initiate the change effort. The energy of the key individual is released to look for ways of sustaining the change. This may involve working with the consultant as to what structures and reward systems may be required to keep the change in place and seeing how other organizations have done it. The focus at this point is on the process of restructuring, rather than the content of the change. This phase is concluded when the key individual has enabled the team to own the sustaining issues and he or she can look at other data and other change issues.

If the key individual is a person whose creativity led to recognizing the need for change in the first place and helping the organization adapt, that same creativity may cause the individual to lose interest by the time the change process comes to the sustaining phase. By the time the end is in sight, the person may lose interest and become bored with getting the organization to sustain the change.

Phase 5 is the critical phase in which, for the first time, some question surfaces of whether it is first-order change or second-order change that is required. The adequacy of the change as perceived and implemented is reviewed in the context of its effects on the long-term perspective of the organization and its ability to engage in continuous change.

CASE: In the religious order, the change process moved the organization to a situation where the strategic plan that had been introduced was being implemented at the local level and was having an impact on the order's relationship with its stakeholders. For example, at one of the order's high schools, there was some reassessment by staff, parents, and alumni regarding the order's new understanding of its mission, and as a consequence a new relationship with the school was initiated.

Phase 6: Follow-through
The Key Individual and the Team Sustaining, the Interdepartmental Group and Organization Doing

The team goes into the sustaining stage when the process for attaining the terminal point of change is defined. The key team defines the end, the phases, time deadlines, who, what, when, and how the change can be sustained. Then it is freed from bearing the burden of change alone as the momentum of change underway carries the change through the entire organization.

If the change process fits the organization's needs, the change gathers momentum that carries it through to the desired end. If the change process is not sufficient to meet the needs for change, if there is a lack of satisfaction within the organization or a lack of ownership of the change process, then the question of whether or not second-order change is required must be dealt with. It is not uncommon, at this point, for an organization facing second-order change to revert to Phase 2 in which the key individual has to convince the key team of the necessity of second-order change and deal with its members' denial and dodging in this regard.

For the religious order, the change process developed a renewed organization in which policy changes and developments were implemented and followed through in its ministries.

Phase 7: Sustaining

The Key Individual, Team, Interdepartmental Group and Organization Sustaining

When there is a new relationship between the organization and peer organizations, when stakeholders come to accept it and interact with it in the new way, and when the structures, reward systems, and review processes are in place, then change is sustained. To sustain change at first, a good deal of energy must be devoted to ensuring the change has worked by monitoring feedback, both from within and outside the organization. Feedback is available through attention to each of the four levels.

After some time, when it is felt that the change is in place and has worked, there is a drop in energy. The organization is moving and it has its own impetus. The organization is fat and happy. Through its normative behavior it reinforces its culture and thereby sets up the mode for future denial (Schein, 1992).

In summary, the seven phases of change provide a framework for one clear fact of experience that is rarely considered in the change literature, namely that in organizational change people change at different paces. This is partly as a result of access to information; the CEO is likely to sense the need for change before others lower in the hierarchy because he has greater access to information. A sales team may be convinced of the need for change from interaction with customers and then have to persuade the top management team to take on the issue. The seven-phases framework is built on the premise that when one party is aware of the need for change and begins initiating change, other parties are typically caught unaware and respond by denying and dodging.

In our consulting and teaching experience, members of organizations can easily recognize what phase their organization is currently in and identify with the prescriptions and issues of each phase. In large organizations sustaining the change process over a period of time across the four levels requires management and knowledge of the terrain. The seven phases give structure to this process.

CASE: The case of the religious order is interesting for two reasons. First, the denying, dodging, and doing stages of change are clearly evident over an eighteen-year period. Each stage lasted several years and required distinctively separate interventions. Second, the three successive regional superiors effectively worked from an organizational levels framework, without being aware of such a framework. Change began with a Level IV strategy intervention, but when that ran into difficulty the key individual turned to intervention on Level I, which naturally flowed into Level II training, and later led to a Level III policy formation process and a Level IV strategic plan. Over the eighteen years, while many first-order changes took place, the deeper second-order, cultural change evolved through the planned change process.

Summary

Change involves a letting go of familiar and accepted ways of seeing and doing things. It can take a lot for us human beings to acknowledge that change is needed. We deny the need for change. Then we dodge it, leaving it to others. When that position cannot be sustained, we begin to see what is required, what needs changing, how, when, and at what cost. As component, incremental changes are made, they need to be sustained so that the overall change survives. This framework adds necessary detail to the Lewin–Schein change model by specifying the initial reactions to change, by showing how members of an organization can be at different stages of the change process because they have access to information others don't have, and by describing how, in an organization, change moves from the key individual, to and through teams, to the group, the entire organization.

The OD consultant can facilitate efforts of the individual manager, the team, the group, and the organization to attend to the processes necessary for change and identify and work through the stages and phases of change (Coghlan, 1989, 1990; Schein, 1987, 1988). A process consultation approach allows the members of an organization to understand what is going on and develop the key diagnostic and problem-solving skills to manage change themselves. The process consultant collaborates with members of the organization in designing the particular activities that help deal with the issues of each stage and move the individual, team, group, and organization through the change phases. This work will be developed in Chapter 8.

7

Phases and Levels of Change in a Communications Company

This chapter considers the case of Long Distance Communications Company (LDC), which had difficulty in managing large-scale communications projects that extended over long distances and long periods of time. These projects began with an analysis of the future communication system demand for each of the point-to-point circuits. Then the circuit paths were chosen by another group, which in turn set up engineering specifications. These specifications were then engineered, land acquired, right of way established, and equipment purchased, installed, tested, and turned over to an operating division. Some 1200 people in twenty groups or functions contributed in a major way to each project to build a new communications link. This case illustrates the phases of complex change through the four levels with the interventions of a consultant.

Phase 1: Disconfirming

Beginning of the Change

During an executive MBA class on the subject of organizational levels, the class was discussing complex change processes in large organizations. One of the students was the vice-president for engineering of LDC. Class discussion centered on large systems change and the difficulties of detecting errors and correcting them over long periods of time in complex projects. The V-P observed that cost overruns on construction projects were causing severe difficulties for his company. Projects would begin with finite funds but at the later stages would lack the necessary resources to make it possible to finish or enable them to work. It was at this stage that the V-P agreed there was a problem. Part of the freedom to admit that a problem existed came from his realization that a solution to the problem was possible. The V-P, as the key individual, moved from denying to dodging at this point.

Contract Setting

Further discussion led the V-P and the consultant, his professor in an executive MBA course, to set up a consultation project for a two-year period to study the project management process. The contract was for process consultation to facilitate the staff's analysis of the problem and to work with the management team to design a self-administered process to solve the problem.

Phase 2: Initiation

The second phase involved the interdepartmental group leaders admitting in their face-to-face working team that problems existed. The five leaders in the interdepartmental group represented every function of engineering, from circuit design to installation engineering. They had the most complete picture of the complex transmission construction process.

Meeting with the Team and Setting the Parameters

The first meeting of the team was most traumatic. The initial reaction was denial that there was a problem, followed by assertion that if there was a problem, it could be solved without a consultant. The consultant was perceived as extra baggage and only tolerated as the V-P's professor. He was someone to be endured but largely ignored. The notion that an outsider be brought into the company was itself a sign of failure and was not to be admitted.

Overcoming Denial

Discussion of the "problem" soon turned technical, and jargon and special engineering language proliferated. The consultant who was to participate as a process observer incidentally had a background in military electronics and began participating in the technical discussion. This caught the team by surprise and brought down some of their defenses. The team slowly accepted the consultant, admitted that a problem existed and began to set out a course of action in which the consultant could play a part. One individual went so far as to suggest that if the consultant had not embarked on a teaching career he might well be working for LDC! The rest concurred. The consultant was, at this point, admitted as a fellow technician and not just a process consultant.

The need for focus soon became apparent. The consultant inquired about the most recently completed circuits and sought to find what could be learned from those projects. The discussion focused on the fact that the projects had been turned over to a group of operators who were to run the equipment providing the communications circuits from point A to point B, and that the people trying to operate it did not have test equipment. The test equipment that was supposed to have been part of the project and necessary for the operations group to use the circuits effectively had not been purchased. The money for their purchase had been spent instead in cost overruns in the early phases of building linkages between point A and point B. Some other operating features designed into the project were also left out due to lack of funds.

Overcoming Dodging

The discussion grew hot and heavy at this point, with every participant wanting to find somewhere to place the blame. Each area was interrogated to see who was at fault. This went on for some time before the consultant intervened.

He set up a make-believe process in which a culprit was chosen to take the blame. The person was asked to get down on his knees and say, "I am sorry." The consultant led the way and showed how to adopt the contrite position. The group was silent for a moment and then began to laugh. The pointlessness of blame was now apparent. Finding the culprits and punishing or shunning them did not solve the problem or change the situation. The interdepartmental group leadership team, in this way, came to process the situation and initiated a plan for the change process.

Phase 3: Maneuvering

The maneuvering phase began with defining the basic problem and outlining the key issues. A systematic analysis had yet to begin. It is the nature of complex processes that no one can see the consequences of his or her actions, yet everyone can see that this is a process in which he or she stands to lose. The defense mechanisms rise quickly.

Getting the Interdepartmental Group Leaders to See the Issues

The second meeting was set up as an all-day meeting. Each person was to bring a large sheet of newsprint, or several, listing all the inputs and outputs from that person's functional area. Traffic analysis would show their hand-offs to the design engineering group. They, in turn, would show their hand-offs to the equipment manufacturers who were not part of the company. The design group would also show the hand-off to the federal relations group for getting permissions and frequency allocations from the Federal Communications Commission (FCC). So it would progress until the five years and the full project was detailed group by group. This process took up the entire morning. The team went to lunch and had a drink to celebrate the morning's success. One member decided to continue the celebration in place of lunch.

A Personal Issue Sets the Interdepartmental Group Leader Back

After the lunch break it was the turn of the individual who had been celebrating to stand before the group for presentation and review. His newsprint had been rolled up during the morning session and was now revealed to be blank. In slurred speech the man told the team angrily that the process was useless, that he did not agree with it and never had, and that he was the most senior and should know what was best. He stormed out of the room. After an awkward silence the remaining team members discussed what was happening. The senior member was a valued individual but over the past year had brought much destruction to the team through abuse of alcohol. His spouse had recently died of cancer and he had begun to drink heavily and to miss work.

It soon became apparent that what the team thought was a team management issue was indeed a personal issue. A meeting was held in which the V-P and some other team members who had the required data confronted the individual and enabled him to seek company-assisted help. The project was put on hold. Distinguishing a Level I issue from a Level II or III issue is difficult at best.

Getting the Interdepartmental Group Leadership Involved in the Change

The next meeting of the interdepartmental group leadership team took place a month later. Leaders of the teams began to put the internal maps together again. Putting the internal maps on paper and talking about the relationships between different functional areas led to emergence of some new information. Some of the hand-off processes, reports that were filed and moved to the next group, were done for functions that no longer existed and were not needed. Obtaining frequency allocations from the FCC was a long and arduous though necessary process for circuits that traveled by microwave. Optic fiber circuits did not radiate a signal and thus had no need for FCC regulations, yet were treated to the FCC allocation process out of habit. The team receiving the report would file it and do nothing with it even though the team members generating it had spent a large amount of time and money preparing it. At this very preliminary stage of internal mapping, problems were soon identified at the intersections between different subfunctions, particularly the hand-offs between those functions. One group's output became another group's input, and the mismatches between those outputs and inputs were very large indeed. The group leadership, reflecting on the internal mapping process, realized the significance of the problem and the extent to which change was required. This analysis only involved the interdepartmental group leaders of Level III. Later meetings with Level II teams revealed that discovery at this level had been only the tip of the iceberg.

Phase 4: Integration

The integration phase has as its basic purpose determining the extent of the problem, the departments the problem involves, and pulling into ownership all the interdepartmental group members required to make the change. For most organizations, this phase covers a large and uncharted area.

An Internal Mapping Process: Gathering the Required Information

All members of the interdepartmental group (numbering about 200) were assembled on a predetermined date, with prior instructions that a detailed list of inputs into their respective functional areas and outputs to adjacent functional areas be produced for a large display. The assembled display would explain the flow of each project from start to finish. This all-day meeting was a complex discussion of detailed inputs and outputs, function by function, area by area, until at the end of the day complex projects extending over five years were detailed. The group could see them from beginning to end. Looking at the mass of information that occupied three of the four walls of a large auditorium, the group was struck by the incredible complexity—well over 1200 hand-offs of technical material of engineering design, blueprints, equipment, requests, or other significant pieces of data were required in the process of each project to construct these communications circuits.

This preliminary exercise made the group realize that *two* different kinds of project were called for. They separated one—an upgrade and renewal project—from the other—the installation of an entirely new channel of communication from point A to point B. Besides accomplishing this analysis, they uncovered some other problem points, such as useless information being prepared for reports that were no longer required due to changes in government regulations. As a result, some modifications of the entire project planning were accomplished and memos were dispatched. Attending to these smaller but significant irritants was the investment of the subordinate team, who now saw the prospective gain from the change process and bought into it.

Change of Vice-President

The vice-president for engineering, who had started this whole process, graduated from the MBA program where his participation in class had triggered the consulting relationship with the firm. He left LDC to become president of another communications company operating on the West Coast. Immediately the search for a successor was initiated by the local company. The person appointed, an engineer by background, had worked in another division of the organization and so was not privy to the change process going on in this division to which he was transferred. He met the group and consultant and discussed the change project and whether or not it was valuable to continue with it. He also joined the same executive MBA program in which his predecessor had participated and was exposed to the construct of levels in classroom discussions. After a lapse of about two months the interdepartmental group was reassembled and the process was focused on two types of projects—an upgrade renewal project and a new communications channel installation project. These two projects would be examples of the rest of the processes within his division. How they would be mapped and the problems found would be indicative of problems in other projects.

Internal Mapping with All the Interdepartmental Group Members

The new V-P brought the group together to begin the internal mapping process with two simplified versions of the project that had been delineated at the previous meetings. Once again, a large auditorium was filled with more than 200 people and its walls with input-output maps of each area and each division juxtaposed with all the other areas or divisions to which there were hand-offs. Lines were drawn from one chart to another and the quality of the input-output transactions was discussed. Sometimes these transactions were annotated as information, at other times as drawings or orders for equipment. The process took two full days. A third day was set aside for a discussion of the action needed and ways to accomplish it. A sense of pride ensued when the overview of the project pointed out to the entire group how complex a process they were about to accomplish.

Phase 5: Action

The action phase took the complex data of the large system and all its interfaces, as mapped, and began defining problem areas, thus enabling change to take place.

Flagging Problems and Forming Repair Teams

After a good deal of discussion with the consultant the group concluded that it needed a way to deal with troublespots. Certain points seemed more critical to some people than to others. A system was set up whereby "flags"—sets of highlighted markers—could be placed anywhere on the displayed project scheme. For a flag to be placed, however, the person who felt that there was a problem had to present the issue to the entire group. After listening to a detailed explanation of the purported problem, the group could agree a problem existed and place a flag, or they could simply clarify the issues at stake. By placing a flag, the group admitted that the area was a point of true dysfunction and they set up a repair team. Anyone who had a stake in what was going to be changed in the course of fixing this problem was included on the repair team. Each team had both a leader and a "flag solver"—the person who had originally placed the flag or had the best description of the dysfunction. The flag solver's judgment would be required for elimination of the flag. At the end of the third working day, twenty-three significant problems had been flagged and repair teams set up.

   Over the next four-month period, flag meetings were held regularly, some weekly and others on a tri-weekly basis. These repair teams were at different levels of the organization's echelon. If a flag was significant enough to cause real disruption in the projects, the team leader may well have been a vice-president. Others were within functional areas in a division with a group manager leading the team.

   At the end of each three-week period an update on the progress of solving each of the flagged problems was prepared and sent out in written form to the entire group. Top management met weekly and reviewed what was happening in the organization, how the change was progressing, and how the repair teams were working. Everyone agreed that the process was having a good effect and that change was taking place. In many instances people realized what was going wrong in flagged problem areas, came up with detailed solutions, and quickly solved the problem without waiting for the entire organization and the next flag meeting.

Phase 6: Follow-through

Burning the Flags

At the end of the first four-month period a ceremonial flag burn-ing was held at an assembly of the entire group. Repair teams presented details, for any completed repair, on how the solution had been found and what action was being taken. The group responded by accepting or rejecting that the problem had been solved. When all parties agreed that a problem was completely solved a small paper flag was placed in a fireproof container and burned. The group cheered that change had come into the system.

Overloading

Early on, the repair teams discovered that other issues seemed to require attention and they afforded them problem-solving time and energy. People saw the opportunity to change the orga-nization and suddenly the repair teams found themselves bur-dened with issues other than the flagged problems on which they were working. Sometimes it was management that added new issues; sometimes it was individuals within the teams. Adding extraneous, incremental change processes had to be nipped in the bud and these were declared to be outside the realm of the change process.

Phase 7: All Sustaining

The sustaining phase was not realized. LDC was restructured and the teams broken up before sustaining processes were in place. Later discussions, after several years had passed, revealed that individuals had taken aspects of the flag process into the new, restructured parts of the organization, however.

Reflection on the Case

We have provided a more extensive case in this chapter in order to illustrate more comprehensively the interaction of the four levels in a complex change situation. It is clear from the case that the progress of the change involved all four levels. The indi-vidual level is evident in the case of the vice-president taking on the change issue and bringing it forward to the team, and then later leaving the company in the interests of his own career. The individual level is also evident in the individual whose alcohol addiction affected the organization's efforts to pursue the problem. The insight that his behavior was a Level I, personal issue rather than a Level II, team management issue was significant.

The entire project involved face-to-face team interaction in identifying problems and generating solutions through both the functional teams and the ad hoc flag teams.

The major thrust for change came through the Level III assemblies, where the systemic picture of the projects was displayed in a manner that enabled the various functional teams and areas to grasp the overall picture and understand the linkages among them. The work of this change project was to enable the company to be more effective in a newly deregulated market. It is also interesting that the key participants found the levels framework a useful construct for understanding the process as it was happening.

The case also illustrates the phases of change described in Chapter 6. The movement from the V-P's denial of the existence of a problem to the interdepartmental group owning the issue and actively seeking solutions demonstrates a complex process of unfreezing from the key individual through the team to the group, with denial and dodging occurring at each point in response to promotion of the change issue. It emphasizes how in a complex change process, although people are exposed to the change question at different stages, they typically respond initially in a denial and dodging mode. We have seen that in this instance denial and dodging can focus on the presence of the consultant and in effect confirm that dodging is taking place. The doing stage comprised detailed work of a complex technical nature over many months, which continued long after the account of this case ends.

The consultant worked in a process consultation mode throughout. His initial interventions stimulated inquiry into the problems being experienced by the company. The critical moment occurred at the first team meeting, when he intervened by demonstrating expertise on the technology at the heart of the firm's business, thus enabling the team to reevaluate his presence and usefulness. This intervention did not negate his process consultation contract, but rather strengthened it. Having gained the management team's trust and respect, the consultant was

then able to re-establish his process consultation role and function as a catalytic agent to facilitate the working of the large
group in both the assemblies and the flag teams. This experience
supports Schein's argument that the process consultant should
not withhold expertise from the client should the client require it
at specific moments, providing that any particular intervention
does not alter the basic process consultation nature of the helping
relationship.

8

Strategies of Intervention

The organizational levels construct is essential for understanding and managing the change process in an organization. Consequently, managing and working with change through the four levels require the consultant and manager to utilize a range of interventions appropriate to the tasks at hand in any given situation. A comprehensive knowledge of the theory and practice of intervention is needed which must be integrated in practice with the understanding of how change can be managed and facilitated within and across the four organizational levels. Effective intervention requires (1) adequate theory in applied behavioral science—organization theory, management, individual psychology, group dynamics, change theory, organization development, and so on—in order to understand the dynamics of change in client systems; (2) a theory of intervention that distinguishes different intervention modes and enables the consultant to choose the best mode for the situation; (3) skills in using different interventions and being able to move from one intervention mode to another as appropriate; and (4) a degree of self-awareness whereby the consultant can reflect in action on the theories he or she is using and on his or her intuitive reactions to what is happening and be able to adapt according to the situation and the needs of the client (Schon, 1983; Nevis, 1987; Schein, 1987; Weisbord, 1987).

A typology of interventions, based on Blake and Mouton's work in OD (1983), provides a valuable and useful approach. The value and usefulness of the Blake and Mouton typology are that, first, it distinguishes different types of intervention in terms of

Table 8.1
Intervention Strategies Across the Four Organizational Levels

	Individual	Face-to-face Team	Interdepartmental Group	Organizational
Acceptant				
Catalytic				
Confronting				
Prescriptive				
Theory/ Principles				

what the consultant or manager actually does, and, second, it provides an essential construct for understanding and selecting an appropriate intervention in a given concrete situation. Blake and Mouton's five interventions—acceptant, catalytic, confronting, prescriptive, and theory/principles—can be applied to the particular tasks and interventions at each of the four organizational levels. Accordingly, the diagrammatic representation is a two-dimensional grid (Table 8.1). In this chapter, we will first outline the Blake and Mouton intervention typology and then apply it to the tasks and issues at each of the four organizational levels to show how the consultant intervenes in order to achieve the goals from the tasks of each level.

Blake and Mouton's Five Intervention Strategies

Acceptant   Acceptant interventions attempt to help a client through active listening when the agenda is fundamentally emotional. This form of intervention is appropriate when feelings and emotions are hampering effectiveness in some way. The intervenor tries to understand the client from the client's point of view, and the client experiences the intervenor's empathy, support, and absence of judgment. The client defines the issues and sets the boundaries. The intervenor accompanies the client through the experience in an accepting and nonjudgmental manner, helping the client clarify and accept feelings, allowing the person the psychological security to talk about the way he or she sees the particular situation. The intervenor does not attempt to move the client toward any resolution. Acceptant interventions are based on the assumptions that when emotion is dominating awareness and experience, attending to it and releasing it is a prerequisite for any further movement. To use another intervention form in this situation blocks the client's release of emotion and frustrates the purpose of the intervention.

Catalytic Catalytic interventions begin at the client's perceived status quo and aim at helping the client improve the way things are done. A catalytic intervention enables the client to determine and fulfill his or her true needs. It assumes that more information about a problem will have a significant input on changing the perception of the problem, and that a focus on the ways and means of gathering information will have an impact. Catalytic interventions are nonauthoritarian. They constitute what are frequently called "facilitative" interventions. The intervenor typically invites the client to define the situation, listens actively, may offer tentative suggestions about how to gather information, supports the client, and encourages the client to make his or her own decisions. Argyris (1970) describes this process in terms of the interventionist having three primary tasks—to help the client generate valid and useful information, to provide the context whereby the client can make a free and informed choice on the basis of that information, and to provide the climate whereby the client is internally committed to that choice of action.

The classical catalytic intervention is the process consultation approach (Schein, 1987, 1988). The consultant promotes the client's engaging in his or her own inquiry by enabling exploration ("Tell me what happened") and understanding ("Why do you think that happened?"). The consultant then facilitates the client's planning and taking action by encouraging the client to explore alternatives and the consequences of particular actions (Schein, 1987; Coghlan, 1990b). Other catalytic intervention methodologies include the specific process consultation methodologies, such as setting an agenda, observing processes and getting feedback, counseling and coaching, and structural interventions. Information may be gathered through interviewing, direct observation, questionnaires and survey instruments, and direct consultant-client interaction (Schein, 1988; Coghlan, 1990b). Catalytic interventions are distinguished from acceptant interventions in that they involve the client in taking responsibility to resolve the problems at issue and facilitate the self-directed change. In this respect, catalytic interventions are more than an intervention strategy; they constitute a philosophy of helping (Schein, 1987, 1988).

Confronting   Values and assumptions direct behavior, generally and specifically. Some values and assumptions are restrictive, rigid, defensive, and lead to self-defeating cycles of behavior. By becoming aware of these a client system has the possibility of reorienting behavior in terms of more valid values. A confronting intervention directly challenges the restrictive attitudes, beliefs, and behaviors of the client. A well-designed confrontation can make the client acknowledge a previously unrecognized contradiction between stated values and behavior. The client is faced with either changing behavior to be more congruent with more valid values or continuing behavior unchanged in the face of the recognized inconsistency. The consultant takes nothing for granted in the reception of the client's description of the situation. The consultant does not impose his or her own values but challenges the client to recognize the assumptions and values behind observable behavior in a way that is nonpunitive and that respects the autonomy of the client to accept or reject the intervention. Confronting interventions need to be selected carefully, as an ill-timed or inappropriate confrontation makes the client defensive and closes down the helping relationship.

Prescriptive   The familiar doctor-patient relationship is the basic prescriptive model of intervention. The patient seeks the doctor's expertise by explaining symptoms and then accepts the doctor's expert diagnosis and subsequent prescription. The assumption is that the patient lacks the necessary knowledge to make a sound self-diagnosis and to design a plan of corrective action. The heart of this intervention strategy is the doctor's expertise. In the consultation arena the focus is on the consultant's expertise: Call in the expert to solve the problem. Prescriptive interventions are more content-focused than process-focused. The content of the consultant's expertise is what is required in the consulting relationship. What is essential in prescriptive intervention is that the prescription be administered in a manner that does not take away the client's autonomy to accept or reject the advice. It is appropriate that expertise and knowledge be handed on, but only where it is requested and in a manner that allows freedom to accept or reject it.

Theory/Principles In the theory/principles intervention mode the client is helped to understand the cause-and-effect variables of a situation through theory-based interventions. The consultant presents relevant theory in a manner that allows the client to accept or reject it. The theory may be presented in general or specific terms. It may be an interpretation of events. Theory is a powerful tool for bringing about change. Hypotheses can be tested and validated. Theory can allow the client to stand back from experience and view it objectively. It can provide a means for communication through a common terminology. The disciplines of psychology, applied behavioral science, organizational theory, group dynamics, and management provide many frameworks for understanding behavior. Indeed, this book is itself a theory intervention in its attempt to articulate an integrated model of organizational behavior and change.

We have presented a typology that distinguishes five forms of intervention—acceptant, catalytic, confronting, prescriptive, and theory/principles. We have not intended to detail each intervention mode further or retrace the ground on the interrelationships between the various intervention modes. That is comprehensively covered by Blake and Mouton (1983). The typology of intervention strategies allows the consultant and manager to distinguish one form of intervention from another and to select the intervention appropriate to a given situation. Clearly, it is rare that any single strategy is the sole intervention needed for any concrete situation. More typically a combination of strategies is employed as appropriate. For instance, if in the initial stages of a consultant's meeting with a client the

client is intensely emotional, the consultant works in an acceptant mode. When, as is often the case, the emotional intensity
subsides, the consultant switches to a catalytic mode by asking
what action the client intends to take. Subsequently, the consultant may utilize the theory/principles mode by offering information, may prescribe action, or may confront the client's attitudes
or intended behavior. Knowledge of the intervention typology
enables the consultant to have a range of interventions from
which to choose and to select interventions that are appropriate
to the client's needs and the issues at hand at a given moment of
a situation. A consultant may move from one intervention mode
to another according to his or her judgment as to what is appropriate and effective. The following Level II case provides a clear
illustration.

CASE: At Transition University the new president invited a process consultant to attend a three-day planning meeting, off-cam-
pus, with himself and his cabinet at the start of the academic
year. This meeting aimed at focusing explicitly on the plans and
issues of each unit within the cabinet—academic affairs, finance,
administrative affairs, student life, development, campus ministry, and the new president's view of the stakeholders in the
university's mission—a Level III and IV agenda. An implicit
agenda was Level II team-building between the new incumbent
and the cabinet of his predecessor. The consultant observed the
process of the meetings and intervened, in a catalytic mode,
regarding clarification, norm formation, leadership style, and
decision-making. A critical part of the three days was judged to
be an evening workshop on the Myers-Briggs Type Indicator
(MBTI). Here the consultant led the group through the Indicator
(a theory intervention), and with the group's permission, charted
the members' perceived types. He then interviewed the president in front of the group on his own perceived strengths and
weaknesses and management style (a confronting intervention
mode). For instance, the president's extroversion was expressed
in his habit of thinking aloud; exploring this habit helped his
staff to clarify whether what he was saying at any moment was
to be taken as an instruction to be implemented or simply thinking aloud. Explorations on the other dimensions of his type were
experienced as fruitful. Through this process the president and
his cabinet began building a working relationship in which

strengths were complemented and areas of frustration identified. This catalytic intervention mode focused attention on the team's process and interpersonal relations and complemented the work done on priorities, goals, and work projects. The consultant subsequently attended some formal meetings on campus as a continuing aid to the team's learning. In this consultation, through a mixture of catalytic, confronting, and theory interventions, issues at Levels II, III, and IV were handled.

Five years later, the president suggested to the consultant that, as there had been a substantial turnover of personnel in the cabinet, it would be useful to rerun the MBTI session at the annual planning meeting. Accordingly, the consultant invited the members to complete the form; some did and others did not. The session itself was somewhat argumentative, with one member dismissing the MBTI as pop psychology and another reporting that a former member claimed that he had been fired because his type was discovered to be different from the president's. The utilization of the MBTI as an intervention in this instance to enable team-building fell flat because (1) the team had not actually requested it but the president had decided that it would be good to do it, and (2) being a theory/principles intervention, it did not meet the client's needs at that time.

A consultant or manager's professional development must include skills at knowing which intervention can best be utilized in a concrete situation and skills in using all five strategies, rather than an overreliance on any one or some. Skill at using each intervention strategy also requires knowledge of how the use of each strategy can degenerate.

Degenerative Interventions

Heron (1990) adds a necessary and very useful sophistication to the intervention strategies' framework by introducing the notions of perverted and degenerative interventions. Perverted interventions are deliberate and malicious and intend to hurt. Degenerative interventions are those that unintentionally fail in their aim to help. One way they fail is through inappropriate category, timing, content, and manner. In other words, someone can give bad advice, or give good advice at the wrong time so that it isn't heard, or give good advice at the right time in a manner that alienates the client so that the advice is not heard.

An inappropriate theory can be utilized or badly communicated. In the context of the organizational levels' framework, intervening on the wrong level, as for instance, team-building when the issue is an interdepartmental group level issue, constitutes a degenerative intervention.

More specific degenerative interventions occur in the use of each category through the consultant or manager's blind, unresolved personal issues or through compulsive, manipulative, or unsolicited interventions. Examples abound in each category. An acceptant intervention is patronizing or ignores difficult issues in situations where the consultant cannot handle strong emotion. A confronting intervention becomes punitive when the consultant doesn't realize that he or she has become angry. A catalytic intervention has degenerated when the consultant asks questions out of curiosity rather than being guided by the needs of the client. Prescriptive interventions are oppressive when the consultant applies excessive moral pressure for his advice to be followed. Theory interventions degenerate when the emphasis shifts to the amount of material the consultant wants to provide rather than the amount that is needed or useful to the client.

Interventions on the Four Organizational Levels

We have argued that a knowledge of intervention theory and practice is essential for the OD consultant and the manager and outlined a typology of intervention strategies so as to ground our presentation of how to intervene in order to achieve the tasks at each of the four organizational levels. Effective intervention requires a choice and skilled use of each of the intervention strategies, particularly in the application of the key intervention on each level that we have presented.

Level I: The Individual Level

On Level I the bonding process by which an individual develops a sense of belonging and loyalty and ultimately integrates personal goals with those of the organization has a significant affective element. Managerial style, organizational culture, organizational procedures, to name just a few aspects, can create loyalty and enthusiasm, indifference or alienation. The individual's developmental task in the concrete reality of life, work, and family cycles can be hampered or facilitated through experience of the workplace. Within an organization, management's task is to match its processes with the human resources at its disposal. The career interview, as the key intervention on this level, is the means whereby the individual locates work experience in the context of his or her whole life. The process of discovering one's career anchor is a process in which an individual is helped by another to locate his or her source of stability in the pattern of career choices (Schein, 1990). For the person in the helping or accompanying role a catalytic stance, with catalytic interventions, is essential. The purpose of the interview is to enable the client take ownership of his or her own life. The individual discovers his/her anchor by engaging in a self-diagnostic activity while his/her companion reflects the pattern in order that the individual can form his/her own judgments. When personal issues surface that generate painful memories or associations, the consultant switches to an acceptant mode, switching back to a catalytic mode at the point when the intensity of the emotion has subsided and the individual is intent on making a decision. The acceptant intervention ceases to be appropriate and is replaced by a catalytic intervention that helps the individual make a decision or take action.

Confronting interventions are sometimes appropriate in the career interview when the consultant sees the need to challenge the individual to examine the relationship between espoused theory and theory-in-use (Argyris, 1990b). There is typically an inconsistency in this relationship. However, as we have already pointed out, confrontation must be used sparingly to avoid eliciting defensiveness. In the career interview, confrontation is appropriate once a trusting relationship has been established and the consultant has utilized core catalytic interventions to the extent that the client feels safe and has taken ownership of the career interview process.

In the process of the career interview the prescriptive intervention would generally not be appropriate. The purpose of the interview is to enable the client to take ownership of his or her own career so as to create appropriate bonding with the organization. Prescriptions regarding specific actions that might contribute to the overall situation are appropriate, however. For example, although it is inappropriate for a consultant to suggest a particular career for an individual, it is appropriate to advise attending a career seminar.

Frequently a relevant theory intervention is made in terms of the dynamics of the adult life, career, and family life cycles (Schein, 1978). The patterns of adult development provide a construct with which the individual grounds particular life, career, and family experiences and gains an understanding of coping mechanisms required to deal with them.

In a career interview, if the client or subordinate becomes emotional because a painful personal issue has surfaced, the manager/consultant can easily slip into a degenerative intervention by reassuring that things will turn out okay. The degeneration occurs through the manager/consultant unwittingly attempting to meet his or her own needs for comfort in the face of the emotion rather than meeting the client's needs. A catalytic intervention degenerates when the consultant, in a quest for valid information, asks too many questions and begins to hound the client in a manner that prompts the client to respond to the questions with yes or no answers and effectively closes down any spirit of inquiry in the client.

The career interview constitutes the key intervention in respect to the bonding task on Level I. For the consultant or manager conducting the interview the intervention typology is immensely useful. While the consultant or manager's dispositions are essentially catalytic, in that he or she is attempting to facilitate the client in his or her own career process, the consultant or manager typically moves from one intervention mode to another in the course of the interview. It is essential to understand that in the context of the career interview, where the interviewee is attempting to assess his or her relationship to the organization in the wider context of his or her life in order to contribute to the matching process between the organization's and personal needs, the different intervention strategies play different roles in achieving the aims of the interview. An inappropriate use of any of the strategies thwarts the process of the interview and negatively affects the bonding process. Accordingly, a critical skill for the consultant is to judge when it is appropriate to use any of the five strategies of intervention and how to use them. In the career interview, use of the catalytic mode is essential and acts as the anchor to the use of the other four strategies.

Level II: The Face-to-Face Team

The key intervention to facilitate the creation of a functioning working team is team-building. The essential approach to team-building by an OD consultant is a catalytic one, whereby the consultant facilitates the team to examine relevant team issues in a way that the team members themselves can perceive, understand, and act upon (Schein, 1988). The catalytic approach to working with teams requires the consultant to differentiate clearly between structuring and nondirectiveness as discrete concepts in order to achieve team self-insight and action (Coghlan and McIlduff, 1990). While the consultant may structure the team's approach to its problem-solving, process review, and decision-making, he does so in a way that allows the team members an opportunity to accept, reject, or modify the consultant's proposed structure.

As shown in Chapter 3, the process consultation framework focuses on task and relational issues under the headings of content, process, and structure. The task issues typically concern setting goals, assigning and accomplishing work, and structures that recur. The relational issues focus on team communication, team roles and functions, team problem-solving and decision-making, team norms, cultural rules of interaction, leadership and authority, and relationship with other teams. A confronting intervention appropriately points out inconsistencies between a team's stated values and its performance or behavior. Particular team functions—task or maintenance roles, leader behavior, norms, the relationship between goals and action—are pinpointed in a confronting manner so the group can assess their dysfunctional role. Acceptant interventions are appropriate when the team members need to listen to each other as a means of healing issues of interpersonal friction. A team may need to resolve interpersonal issues that arise from the leader's style, differences in psychological type, inadequate communication procedures, and dysfunctional behavior. The focus of the acceptant intervention is the active listening of team members to one another. Prescriptive interventions are utilized when the consultant structures particular forms of team-building activities, as when an off-site retreat is set up or a format for a meeting or workshop is designed.

CASE: A bishop set up a committee, comprising clergy, laity, and nuns, to formulate a pastoral plan for his diocese. The committee was to engage in social analysis, reflect on the information gathered in the light of Christian values, involve other groups and structures within the diocese, and then provide training and education for people in the diocese on how to determine needs, view them in terms of Christian mission, and take collective action as a Christian community. In this respect this committee functioned as a parallel learning structure as it attempted to work in a manner that reflected the values it espoused so as to provide a role model for other groups in the diocese (Bushe and Shani, 1991).

Each year, the committee engaged a process consultant for a two-day meeting to help it review its process and maintain the team. On one occasion the committee reported experiencing a great deal of frustration working in the wider system of the diocese. Although, on the one hand they had great personal support from the bishop, on the other hand it was difficult to gain access to and credibility with the local pastors in the mainstream hierarchical structure of the diocese. The consultant worked in an acceptant mode as committee members voiced feelings of frustration and moved to a catalytic mode as he facilitated the committee's exploration of ways to deal with these issues. The consultant presented some theory on the dynamics of middle groups, those groups set up to manage policy that find themselves located between the top management that sets policy and the lower hierarchical groups that have clearly defined tasks, and he illustrated how frustration is inherent in such groups (Fry, Rubin, and Plovnick, 1981). This theoretical input freed the committee from the emotional block of its frustration and the members began to plan how to work more effectively, given their newfound understanding of the inherent frustration in the committee's role as a middle group. The consultant then reverted to the catalytic intervention mode.

Level III: The Interdepartmental Group Level

There is a basic catalytic ingredient to the internal mapping process on the interdepartmental group level. A consultant can facilitate the gathering of information relevant to the situation in need of change by mapping work flow, information exchanges, and issues of the use of scarce resources, and can structure the situation so that the heads of particular functions meet and examine the dysfunctioning that is occurring on this level. We have described such a process extensively in the case presented in Chapter 7.

We argued that knowledge of content is essential when working on Level III. Because a consultant helps Level III reconfigure its information and its materials-handling processes for possible restructuring in an internal mapping intervention, expertise in the content of the problem is fundamental. The consultant must be conversant with the content of the technology in an information flow or decision-making process. The consultant's advice and prescription are central to the solving of technological and structural dysfunction. We saw in Chapter 7 that the consultant's knowledge of electronics not only gave him some level of credibility with his clients but was significant at the later developments of the process when the amount of information increased considerably and became more and more complex and technical.

Level IV: The Organizational Level

On the organizational level a catalytic approach is key to the open systems planning activity (Beckhard and Harris, 1987). The consultant provides the framework whereby the organization engages in analysis of its domains in terms of present and future demands and responses. The consultant facilitates the identification of significant stakeholder groups, switching to a theory/principles intervention mode on the function and role of stakeholders when appropriate. Similarly regarding strategy and policy, constructs for understanding the environment and the market are essential. Hax and Majluf (1991) summarize many of the analytic frameworks that are useful in the strategic planning and strategic management processes.

In an open systems planning meeting, a CEO unwittingly slipped into using the term "shareholders" rather than "stakeholders" in his presentation of the major issues facing the organization. This created some confusion among those present at the meeting and individuals began to query how particular groups could be viewed as shareholders. The consultant intervened by confronting the CEO in his use of terminology, clarified the distinction between stakeholders and shareholders (a theory/principles intervention), and facilitated a discussion of the notion of stakeholders as key demands groups for the organization to take account of in its strategic planning.

The dysfunction of self-defeating cycles is more acute. Organizations can manifest policies and behavior that develop from very suspect assumptions and strategies (Argyris, 1990b). These assumptions or governing variables have behavioral consequences, which in turn affect organizational effectiveness. For example, reports that take too much time and resources are not read or used. On Level IV dysfunctions are based on outside interaction with customers, markets, and competition. The task on Levels III and IV is to confront those assumptions so that the organization can learn and develop skills of adaptive coping (Schein, 1980).

Using Intervention Strategies

In this chapter we have argued that (1) the typology of interventions, based on Blake and Mouton's work in OD (1983), provides a valuable and useful approach in distinguishing different types of intervention in terms of what the consultant or manager actually does, and providing an essential construct for understanding and selecting an appropriate intervention in a given concrete situation, and (2) Blake and Mouton's five interventions—acceptant, catalytic, confronting, prescriptive, and theory/principles—are relevant to the particular tasks and interventions at each of the four organizational levels. The following case provides an illustration of where the issue of organizational levels and interventions were not clarified sufficiently for an effective intervention to occur.

CASE: A high school faculty wished to formulate a five- to ten-year plan to replace the ten-year plan that was reaching the end of its term and engaged two consultants to facilitate the process. The consultants were in contact initially with the principal and then met the faculty's representative council to hear what was wanted. The process was to be structured around three single days that were to be spread over a nine-month period. For the consultants the contract was perceived as a Level IV task creating a strategic plan that would position the high school in its environment according to its mission. Content of the intervention would be engaging the faculty in a Level II team-building process through attention to goals and mission, decision-making, and planning implementation; process was the *way* the faculty engaged in these issues. The consultants would work in a process consultation approach.

The consultants designed a structure and process and submitted it to the representative council for approval. The theme of the first day was the question, "Where have we come from?" The faculty would review the experience of the past ten years, list successes and failures, and determine what had been learned from implementing the previous plan, focusing on patterns that would be relevant and applicable for a new plan. The second day would be structured around the question, "Who are we now?" and would employ the core steps of the open systems planning process—identifying current stakeholders, their demands, and the school's current responses and identifying future stakeholders and their demands. The third day would focus on the planning process out of the results of the other two days in terms of the question, "Where are we going?"

The reply came back that the structure of the first day's work did not contain sufficient material and that the faculty thought that not enough progress would be made that day, as, it was argued, the faculty had been through this before, was very experienced at "this sort of thing," and could move expeditiously through a lot of the material. Accordingly, the consultants redesigned the first day so as to cover the process of retrospection and assessment of the present. On the day itself the consultants worked in a catalytic manner—structuring the day, asking questions, writing up answers, drawing material together, encouraging the participants—with some prescription—prescribing small group discussions and tasks. There was some use of confrontation, for example, when the material was gathered, one of the consultants reflected that there was a notable absence of negative issues listed. On other occasions the consultant asked direct questions as to how controversial issues would be dealt with and how confident participants felt in dealing with them.

In general, the consultants felt pleased with the day; the past had been reviewed and the present values and concerns listed for insertion into the next stage. Some difficult areas had been identified and flagged for special consideration and the foundation for the next step had been well constructed.

Some weeks later the consultants were invited to a lunchtime meeting with the representative council. At the outset the position was stated clearly; the members of the faculty were unhappy with the day's work. They had done a lot of work and the consultants had drawn very little out of it. It emerged that there had been difficulties in some of the small groups where dysfunctional behavior by individuals had disrupted the work, and that a veiled attack on the principal by a senior member had upset many of the faculty. The result was that the faculty no longer had confidence in the consultants and were terminating the contract.

This case can be reviewed through two interdependent approaches. First, on a Level II face-to-face team or on a Level III collection of departments. We can review it in terms of organizational levels and ask how to approach working with a client system such as a school faculty. Is a faculty a Level II face-to-face team or is it a Level III interdepartmental group? Academic faculties in high schools and other institutions of learning do not form face-to-face teams in the manner of commerce or service organizations, other than in committees and when working as faculty boards (Rashford and Coghlan, 1992). Teaching is essentially solo work and collegial relationships or a team form around administrative issues, which many academics would perceive as secondary to their main work of research and teaching. Despite the appearances and assertions that the high school faculty were a single working unit, it was mistaken to approach the task in those terms. It would have been more appropriate to approach the task in terms of working with a Level III configuration of coalitions and interests, which would have to negotiate areas of common ground. In such a frame of reference the consultants' approach would need to have been different. Their catalytic interventions would need to have been focused on the basis for forming consensus, with theory/principles directed more toward forming consensus in political coalitions and showing how the strategy designed would lead to that result, and confrontation and acceptant interventions used to deal with the specific feelings and issues that would emerge as the process unfolded.

The consultants' interventions were not adequate. While the consultants worked in a catalytic mode they did not provide sufficient theory or principles to explain what was happening, where the process was going, and how particular steps in the process fitted together to enable the faculty to achieve its goal of formulating a strategic plan. The faculty as a group appeared to be operating in a dependency-flight mode, where (1) it was unable not only to confront the dysfunctioning of some of its own members but also to acknowledge that the small group processes had been difficult, and (2) it had the largely unarticulated expectation that the consultants would know everything that was going on and would sort it out (Hirschhorn, 1991). The stated position that the faculty had been through all this before, had a wealth of experience and competence in working in small groups and moving forward, and so could move quickly through the early stages of the strategic planning process was unfulfilled. The consultants' intervention strategies did not enable these hidden psychological issues to emerge.

From the consultants' viewpoint the venture collapsed for two reasons: First, they had assumed incorrectly that the primary work would be with a Level II face-to-face working team, which would integrate around common goals and operate as a single unit, whereas it emerged that the faculty was more a Level III configuration of interests and coalitions that would have to work to create common ground. Second, their interventions failed to meet the client's needs as the process unfolded, and because those needs remained unarticulated, the consultants failed to enable the faculty have a positive experience that it was making relevant progress.

Summary

In this chapter we have focused on the theory and practice of intervention in relation to achieving the tasks on the four organizational levels. We introduced the Blake and Mouton typology of five intervention strategies—acceptant, catalytic, confronting, prescriptive, and theory/principles—and argued that it is valuable and useful because it distinguishes different types of intervention in terms of what the consultant or manager actually does, and it provides an essential construct for understanding and selecting an appropriate intervention in a given concrete situation.

We then applied the typology to the tasks and issues at each of the four organizational levels to show how the consultant intervenes in order to achieve the goals from the tasks of each level. In this regard we have argued that, while the catalytic mode is an essential philosophy of helping a client system help itself (Schein, 1987, 1988; Coghlan, 1989, 1990b) and acts as an anchor to all other interventions at each of the levels, the other four intervention modes can be utilized in conjunction and harmony with it.

Effective intervention requires that the appropriate intervention mode be utilized in a concrete situation with the particular tasks and interventions at each of the four organizational levels. Knowing at which level one is working is an essential diagnostic skill for the consultant or manager. Choice of intervention must follow from an understanding of the level of the issues under consideration so that the intervention itself may facilitate development or resolution of the relevant issues or task, on the individual, team, interdepartmental group, or organizational level.

9

Integration

We have presented the notion of the four organizational levels as a comprehensive framework for linking the multiple dynamics of organizational life and change. The relationship between individual and organization, the individual participating in the team, the team's contribution to the group, and the interdepartmental group's role in the organization's survival and success through the key tasks of bonding, creating a functioning productive team, coordination, and adaptation form a complex systemic pattern (Table 9.1). This pattern provides a significant diagnostic tool for understanding the many issues that occur in organizations and for clarifying the complexities of organizational change.

The Adaptive Coping Cycle

The process whereby information is received into an organization, processed, and transformed into output is described by Schein in terms of a cycle of continuous coping (Schein, 1980). In order that organizations remain adaptive to the changing environment, they require: an ability to take in and communicate information reliably and validly; internal flexibility and creativity to make the changes that are demanded by the information obtained; integration of and commitment to the multiple goals of the organization, from which comes the willingness to change when necessary; an internal climate of support and freedom from threat; and the ability to continuously redesign the structure to be congruent with their goals and tasks. The following

Table 9.1
Tasks at Each of the Four Organizational Levels

Level	Task
I. Individual	Bonding
II. Face-to-face team	Creating a working team
III. Interdepartmental group	Coordinating
IV. Organizational	Adapting

sequence of activities constitutes an organization's adaptive coping cycle. It begins with a change in some aspect of the organization's internal or external environment and ends with a more adaptive, dynamic equilibrium for dealing with the change.

There are five stages in the adaptive coping cycle.

1. Sensing a change in some part of the internal or external environment

2. Importing the relevant information about the change into those parts of the organization that can act upon it and digesting the implications of that information

3. Changing production or conversion processes inside the organization according to the information obtained, while reducing or managing undesired side effects in related systems and stabilizing the change

4. Exporting new products or services that are more in line with the originally perceived changes in the environment

5. Obtaining feedback on the success of the change through further sensing of the state of the external environment and the degree of integration of the internal environment.

As Schein points out, an organization can have dysfunctions on any of these five steps. It can fail to sense changes in the environment or it can misinterpret them. It can fail to transmit the relevant information to those parts of the system that can act upon it. The information may fail to affect the production or conversion processes so that change takes place. A change may not result in a renewed output or there may be inadequate feedback of the effect of the changed product or service on the client or customer that enables the organization to reassess its strategic role and function. Each of the steps requires specific attention in order that the organization adapt successfully to a changing environment.

Organizational Levels, Adaptive Coping, and Organizational Change

Schein's adaptive coping cycle parallels the stages of change and can be framed as a change or organization development cycle (Fig. 9.1). The sensing of information and importing into the system involves disconfirmation. The system won't deal with it until it has worked through its anxiety and sufficient psychological safety has been created. The processes of digesting the infor-

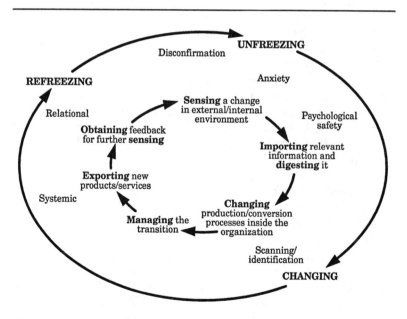

Figure 9.1
The Adaptive Coping Cycle and the Change Process

mation and changing production or conversion processes and managing the transition require scanning for appropriate solutions, with the possible use of an OD consultant. Systemic refreezing occurs when the change fits the organization and is integrated into the internal system and the relational external environment.

We have added "managing the transition" as an additional stage to the adaptive coping cycle. The primary task in a change situation is to move from the present to the future by assessing the present in terms of a hypothetical future so as to determine the work to be done. Between the present and the future states is the transition state, which according to Beckhard must be perceived as a unique state in need of conscious management (Beckhard and Harris, 1987; Beckhard and Pritchard, 1992; Coghlan 1990a). There are two aspects to managing this transition state. One is to identify the relevant tasks and activities to bring about the change. This is the doing/changing stage, involving planning and implementing action. An activity plan is simply the identification of the forms of activities, structures, projects, and experiments that will help achieve the desired state. The second aspect of transition management is to set up the structures and mechanisms necessary to accomplish those tasks. As no amount of change can take place without commitment, the planners of the change develop a plan to elicit that commitment. Such a plan focuses on the persons who must be committed to the change if it is to happen. This involves effective responses to issues of denying and dodging across Levels I, II, and III.

As Chapter 6 showed, the process of change involves a movement of the change issue through the four organizational levels. The change process begins with an individual coping initially with data that demand change by denying and dodging before doing by carrying the issue through other individuals to the key individual. The key individual, having passed through the denial and dodging stages, takes the idea to the team, which, after its own denying and dodging, takes it to the interdepartmental group, and so on. This process adds detail and sophistication to the adaptive coping cycle and illustrates the complexity in the organizational adaptive coping cycle in terms of both the content of the change and of the relational process through the four levels (Fig. 9.2).

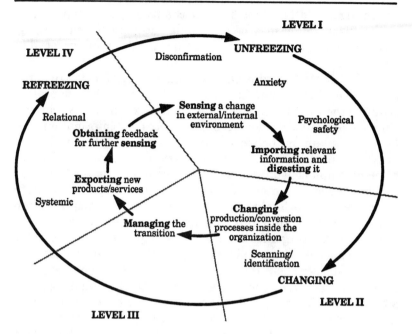

Figure 9.2
Organizational Levels, Adaptive Coping, and Organizational Change

Change Across the Four Organizational Levels

The interrelationship and interdependence of the four organizational levels become yet more focused and intense in a situation of organizational change. Systemic organizational change, whereby an organization attempts to adapt to changing environmental demands, necessitates a realignment of the group's coordination, the teams' functioning, and the bonding process of individuals to a changing or changed organization.

An organization's *unfreezing* involves the unfreezing of key individuals, the application of key teams to the question of the need for change, and the generalization of the change agenda to the interdepartmental group. At each of these levels denial and dodging have to be dealt with in order to take the organization to the doing stage. At the doing stage, while those leading the change are attempting to make change happen, many others in the organization may be struggling with denial and dodging. The sequential nature of this process was presented in detail in Chapter 6.

In a situation of organizational change that is triggered by external environmental forces, the task of adaptation requires the interdepartmental group to reconfigure its relationships—the reallocation of resources, access to information, collective bargaining between management and trade unions, denial and dodging in the context of interteam politics. Managers and consultants must be able to diagnose when critical issues require intervention at this third level, and able to intervene appropriately to enable the interdepartmental group to maintain its coordinating function within the organization.

Complex organizational change requires teams to reset goals, reallocate work, and appropriately review process and ensure interpersonal relationships within the team are not adversely affected by the change process. Denial and dodging in a team typically lead to blaming and can create serious disruption. This is a common focus for diagnosis and intervention by managers and consultants as they facilitate team-building as a significant element in an organization's change process. What is essential for the consultant and the manager is that team-building be recognized and utilized as a mechanism for resolving Level II team issues—creating a functional working team, and not the somewhat inevitable, generic tool for change. The organizational levels framework aims at enabling managers and consultants to distinguish the tasks and issues at each of the four levels and intervene appropriately. Team-building and particular interventions within team-building attempt to resolve issues of a face-to-face functioning nature and need to be distinguished from those of an individual (Level I) or interdepartmental group (Level III) nature.

Large-scale organizational change has an impact on individuals in an organization. Some may lose their jobs and be forced to leave the organization. Some remain in the organization, but with reduced status (perceived or real) or working in a different section of the organization or doing different work. For some this changed state is perceived as exciting, challenging, and a force for development and advancement; for others it is perceived as threatening and demeaning and results in a lessening of motivation, self-esteem, and self-confidence.

The bases for reacting to change by individuals are numerous and profound and beyond the scope of this discussion. However, as described earlier, it is acknowledged that as there is an integral link between an individual's participation in organizational life and the tasks and issues of the adult life, work, and family cycles, any forced realignment of an individual's position in an organization demands specific attention (Schein, 1978). Accordingly, triggering events on Level IV, which set off a chain of change on Levels III and II must be dealt with on Level I also. The changing or changed organization is viewed by the individual through the lenses of the life, work, and family cycles and evaluated from that perspective. The consequence is that an increase or decrease in an individual's sense of bonding in the organization is effected. The individual may feel more involved, enthusiastic, and committed to the changed organization or may feel alienated and demotivated. Denial and dodging may predominate and lock the individual in a mode where unfreezing increasingly becomes more painful and threatening.

Consequently managers and consultants are required to follow through the change process by recognizing (1) the interdependent nature of what takes place on Levels IV, III, and II with the individual's sense of bonding, and (2) that the specific nature of bonding issues is distinguished from those of the face-to-face team or interdepartmental group coordination. Consequently interventions directed at meeting bonding issues are an essential and necessary part of the change process.

Organizational Learning

Adaptive coping is one element of survival. A second element is the learning that enables generation and creativity to take place. Senge (1990) points out that the real leverage in most management situations lies in understanding dynamic complexity rather than detail complexity and argues that a shift of thinking to a systemic one that considers complex patterns of relationships rather than linear cause and effect is required in order to manage complexity more effectively. In his view, such systemic thinking is the basis for organizational learning. Accordingly, he presents the five disciplines necessary for organizational learning and outlines how each discipline can contribute to generative learning. Senge's five disciplines are personal mastery, mental models, shared vision, team learning, and systems thinking. Each of these five disciplines benefits from an understanding and use of the four organizational levels.

"Personal mastery" is grounded on the individual level and marks the individual in the process of understanding, choosing, deepening personal goals through the life-cycle in dialogue with the organization's management. Some of the cases cited through the book have illustrated the failure of personal mastery (the manager whose alcoholism crippled his ability to function or Howard Head's blindness to seeing what was happening organizationally in the Head Ski Company).

"Mental models" are central to the functioning of each level. The process of uncovering and acknowledging "theories-in-use" and cultural assumptions constitutes understanding the task and relational structures on each level, as shown in Chapter 3. These structures comprise assumptions about work and work motivation, organizational skills and desires on Level I, standard operating procedures and recurrent interpersonal relationships and roles on Level II, assumptions around resource and information sharing and interteam and group subcultures on Level III, and the organizational self and environmental images on Level IV. Head's mental model of running a company clashed with the skills necessary to run an organization with the result that he lost his company. The university president used his cabinet to transform the mental model of leadership in the cabinet itself and though it across the university.

"Shared vision" is a central element grounding each of the four levels. It contributes to the bonding process on Level I, the building of working functional teams on Level II, the coordination of multiple teams on Level III, and the organization's unified strategic posture on Level IV. The pharmaceutical labs focused its efforts on reaching a shared vision of the company's mission and the subsequent coordination of effort across the four levels built on that focus.

"Team learning" is more specific to Levels II and III and has consequences for Levels I and IV. In the Head Ski Company the absence of team reflection and learning between Head and Siegal, and the ways that conflict was played out in the relations among the departments were ultimately destructive to the company. In the Transition University case, the new president recognized the need for team learning and focused attention on process. The president's own role with regard to process, the occasional presence of the process consultant, attempts to build in process reflection on the team's progress on a monthly basis, and rotating facilitation of team meetings by members illustrate different approaches to enable the team to adapt to a participative culture, not only in the president's cabinet but in their own functional teams and throughout the university.

"Systems thinking" pervades the construct of the four organizational levels, which is itself a systems framework. The essential link between each level, as discussed in Chapter 4, demonstrates how the relationship between levels is both a cause and an effect—that is, events of Level I can cause events on Level II and also be the effect of events on Level II. The interrelationships across the four levels are not simply linear; the feedback loops travel in both directions. Each level is held in place by the other levels and, as we have seen, the systemic interrelationship between levels is particularly highlighted in a change situation. As discussed in Chapter 6 the change process in a complex social system requires individuals to cross boundaries in the organization's echelon and on the four levels described in this book. The process of crossing boundaries between the four levels is rarely examined in the literature, other than from the psychoanalytical perspective (Rice, 1990; Kets de Fries and Associates, 1991). The systemic nature of the interrelatedness and interdependence of our framework of the four organizational levels strengthens our understanding of organizations and of the process of large systems change by delineating the tasks of each level and constructing the systemic relationships between them as was done in Chapter 4. The Head Ski Company illustrates the systemic nature of the levels framework. Howard Head's Level I issues affected his Level II team, the Level III group, and the organization's survival. When the bottom of the early aluminum skis fell out, that product failure affected the organization's credibility in the market, Head's discomfort with Siegal, and Head's view of his own role in the organization. Each of the events on each level described in the case both cause and are affected by events on the other levels. The framework of the four levels of organizational behavior is a genuine systemic framework.

Conclusions

The organizational levels framework constitutes a clinical diagnostic tool whereby the multiplicity of issues that occur in an organization can be viewed through the lenses of the four levels. We have seen in the many examples throughout the book that some organizational problems can be diagnosed in terms of individual bonding, some in terms of face-to-face team functioning, some in terms of interdepartmental group coordination, and others in terms of organizational adaptation. Accurate diagnosis of the nature of problems under consideration is essential for intervention. Any intervention requires a knowledge of intervention theory, a grounding in the interventions appropriate for each level and between levels, and the skills to use them.

The construct of organizational levels has its conceptual foundations in macro- and micro-organizational theory, and complements the extensive literature on the individual in the organization as well as literature on human resource management, team dynamics, interdepartmental group coordination (information technology, decision support systems, interteam dynamics, and industrial relations) strategic planning and management, and organizational change and development. The construct strengthens the clinical literature on how individuals, groups, and organizations change and how people in complex social and technological systems manage change.

Adaptive and learning organizations are built on the integration of the four levels—the individual and the organization in appropriate bonding, functioning and productive teams, the coordination of resources, information, and technology, the multiple teams that form the interdepartmental group, and skills at adaptation to meet environmental demands, both internal and external.

Complex change in an organization can take several years. It is difficult for an individual or a team to see clearly what is happening at any point of a large-scale change without a schema that is a coherent and systemic map of the period and puts the process into perspective. The frustration and apparent lack of solution that, when it is evident that a change process is proving to be inadequate and second-order change is called for, becomes comprehensible using organizational levels and change theory.

The seven-phase schema by which change moves through an organization across the four levels is essential for understanding and managing the typical complex interweaving of information-sharing, reactions from individuals, team meetings for problem-analysis and decision-making, interdepartmental group meetings, and collective bargaining as the organization's management works to transfer disconfirming information into a renewed organization in light of its mission and desired future state.

As organizations face continuous adaptation to external and internal forces the framework of four organizational levels, as it distinguishes issues of individual bonding from those of face-to-face team functioning, interdepartmental group coordination, or organizational adaptation, provides a necessary and useful construct for managers, consultants, and teachers of organizational behavior to understand what is happening and what interventions may be needed in a change process in order that to integrate change throughout an organization.

References

Alderfer, C. P. 1976. Change Processes in Organizations. In M. Dunnette (Ed.) *Handbook of Industrial and Organizational Psychology.* Chicago: Rand McNally.

Allen, T. 1977. *Managing the Flow of Technology.* Cambridge, MA: MIT Press.

Ancona, D., and Caldwell, D. 1988. Beyond Task and Maintenance: Defining External Functions in Groups. *Group and Organization Studies,* 13(4), 468–494.

Argyris, C. 1970. *Intervention Theory and Method.* Reading, MA: Addison-Wesley.

———. 1990a. *Integrating the Individual and the Organization,* with a New Introduction by the author. New Brunswick, NJ: Transaction.

———. 1990b. *Overcoming Organizational Defenses.* Boston: Allyn and Bacon.

Barrett-Lennard, G. T. 1991. A Person-Centered Systemic Model of Change. *Paper presented at The Second International Conference on Client-Centered and Experiential Psychotherapy.* Scotland: Stirling.

Bartunek, J. M., and Louis, M. R. 1988. The Interplay of Organization Development and Organizational Transformation. In W. A. Pasmore and R. W. Woodman, *Research in Organizational Change and Development, Vol. 2:* Greenwich, CN: JAI Press.

Bartunek, J. M., and Moch, M. 1987. First-order, Second-order and Third-order Change and Organization Development: A Cognitive Approach, *Journal of Applied Behavioral Science,* 23(4), 483–500.

Beckhard R. 1972. Optimizing Team Building Efforts. *Journal of Contemporary Business,* 1(3), 23–32.

Beckhard, R., and Harris, R. 1987. *Organizational Transitions: Managing Complex Change,* 2d ed. Reading, MA: Addison-Wesley.

Beckhard, R., and Pritchard, W. 1992. *Changing the Essence: The Art of Creating and Leading Change in Organizations.* San Francisco: Jossey-Bass.

Belbin, R. M. 1981. *Management Teams: Why They Succeed or Fail.* London: Heinemann.

Blake, R., and McCanse, A. 1991. *Leadership Dilemmas—Grid Solutions.* Houston: Gulf.

Blake, R., and Mouton, J. 1983. *Consultation,* 2d ed. Reading, MA: Addison-Wesley.

Bunker, B., and DeLisle, J. 1991. Individual Change in Organizational Settings. In R. C. Curtis and G. Stricker (Eds.), *How People Change: Inside and Outside Therapy.* New York: Plenum.

Bushe, G., and Shani, A. B. 1991. *Parallel Learning Structures.* Addison-Wesley: Reading, MA.

Coghlan, D. 1987. Corporate Strategy in Catholic Religious Orders. *Long Range Planning,* 20(1), 44–51.

———. 1989. OD Interventions in Catholic Religious Orders. In R. N. Ottaway (Ed.), Innovative Organization Development Practices, Part 1, *Journal of Managerial Psychology,* 4(4), 4–6.

———. 1990a. Managing Apostolic Change. *Human Development,* 11(2), 23–27.

———. 1990b. Process Consultation in a Voluntary Youth Organization. *Organization Development Journal,* 8(1), 36–41.

Coghlan, D., and McIlduff, E. 1990. Structuring and Nondirectiveness in Group Facilitation. *Person-Centered Review,* 5(1), 13–29.

Coghlan, D., and Rashford, N. S. 1991. Developing Key Intervention Skills on Four Organizational Levels. In J. Bigelow (Ed.), *Managerial Skills: Explorations in Practical Knowledge.* Newbury Park, CA: Sage.

Fox, A. 1985. *Man Mismanagement.* London: Hutchinson.

Freeman, R. E. 1984. *Strategic Management: A Stakeholder Approach.* Marshfield, MA: Pitman.

French, W., and Bell, C. 1990. *Organization Development,* 4th ed. Englewood Cliffs, NJ: Prentice-Hall.

Friedlander, F., and Schott, B. 1981. The Use of Task Groups and Task Forces in Organizational Change. In R. Payne and C. L. Cooper, *Groups at Work.* Chichester: Wiley.

Fry, R., Rubin, I., and Plovnick, M. 1981. Dynamics of Groups that Execute or Manage Policy. In R. Payne and C. L. Cooper, *Groups at Work.* Chichester: Wiley.

Greiner, L., and Schein V. E. 1988. *Power and Organization Development.* Reading, MA: Addison-Wesley.

Harrison, M. 1987. *Diagnosing Organizations.* Newbury Park, CA: Sage.

Hax, A. C., and Majluf, N. S. 1991. *The Strategy Concept and Process.* Englewood Cliffs, NJ: Prentice-Hall.

Heron, J. 1990. *Helping the Client.* London: Sage.

Hirschhorn, L. 1991. *Managing in the New Team Environment.* Reading, MA: Addison-Wesley.

Kakabadse, A., and Parker, C. (Eds.) 1984. *Power, Politics and Organizations: A Behavioural Science View.* Chicester: Wiley.

Kets de Fries, M., and Associates. 1991. *Organizations on the Couch: Clinical Perspectives on Organizational Behavior and Change.* San Francisco: Jossey-Bass.

Kolb, D., Rubin, I., and McIntyre, J. 1984. *Organizational Psychology: An Experiential Approach,* 4th ed. Englewood Cliffs, NJ: Prentice-Hall.

Leavitt, H. 1979. *Managerial Psychology,* 4th ed. Chicago: University of Chicago Press.

Levy, A. 1986. Second-Order Planned Change: Definition and Conceptualization. *Organizational Dynamics,* Summer, 4–20.

Lewin, K. 1951. *Field Theory in Social Science, Collected Papers of Kurt Lewin,* ed. D. Cartwright. New York: Harper and Row.

Likert, R. 1961. *New Patterns of Management.* New York: McGraw-Hill.

Lippitt, R., Watson, J., and Westley, B. 1958. *The Dynamics of Planned Change.* New York: Harcourt, Brace and World.

McGregor, D. 1960. *The Human Side of Enterprise.* New York: McGraw-Hill.

Miller, J. G. 1978. *Living Systems.* New York: McGraw-Hill.

Nevis, E. C. 1987. *Organizational Consulting: A Gestalt Approach.* Cleveland: Gestalt Institute of Cleveland Press.

Ottaway, R. N. 1983. The Change Agent: A Taxonomy in Relation to the Change Process. *Human Relations,* 30(4), 361–392.

Porter, M. 1980. *Competitive Strategy.* New York: Basic Books.

Pugh, D. 1986. Organizational Development Strategies. In *Planning and Managing Change, Open University Course Guide,* Milton Keynes: Open University.

Rashford, N. S., and Coghlan, D. 1992. Effective Administration through Organizational Levels. *Journal of Educational Administration,* 30(4), 63–72.

Reddy, W. B., and Jamison, K. (Eds.) 1988. *Team Building: Blueprints for Productivity and Satisfaction.* Alexandria, VA–San Diego, CA: NTL Institute-University Associates.

Rice, A. K. 1990. Individual, Group and Intergroup Processes. In E. Trist and H. Murray (Eds.), *The Social Engagement of Social Science, Vol. 1, The Socio-Psychological Perspective.* London: Free Association Books.

Rousseau, D. 1985. Issues in Organizational Research: Multi-level and Cross-level Perspectives. In L. L. Cummings and B. M. Staw (Eds.), *Research in Organizational Behavior, Vol. 7.* Greenwich, CN: JAI Press.

Schein, E. H. 1961. *Coercive Persuasion.* New York: Norton.

———. 1978. *Career Dynamics: Matching Individual and Organizational Needs.* Reading, MA: Addison-Wesley.

———. 1980. *Organizational Psychology,* 3d ed. Englewood Cliffs, NJ: Prentice-Hall.

———. 1987. *Process Consultation, Vol. 2: Lessons for Managers and Consultants.* Reading, MA: Addison-Wesley.

———. 1988. *Process Consultation, Vol. 1: Its Role in Organization Development,* 2d ed. Reading, MA: Addison-Wesley.

———. 1990. *Career Anchors: Discovering Your Own Values,* 2d ed. San Diego: University-Associates.

———. 1992. *Organizational Culture and Leadership,* Rev. Ed. San Francisco: Jossey-Bass.

Schon, D. 1983. *The Reflective Practitioner.* New York: Basic Books.

Senge, P. 1990. *The Fifth Discipline.* New York: Doubleday.

Weisbord, M. 1987. *Productive Workplaces.* San Francisco: Jossey-Bass.